Who's Who in Kentucky Arts and Crafts©

2006 Annual Edition

By Arlene Wright-Correll

An Annual Yearbook of Kentucky Artists and Crafters

Here you will find every type of KY artist and crafter interviewed in 2006, discover their art; learn about them and how to locate them.

This book is dedicated to all the Kentucky artists and crafters who made this work possible. Thanks for giving me your time and information to share with others and we wish you great sales!

Front cover "Zen Poppies©" by Arlene Wright-Correll

ISBN- 978-0-6151-4755-0

Publications Trade Resources Unlimited

100 Dave Wintsch Rd., Munfordville, KY 42765 (270) 524 9567

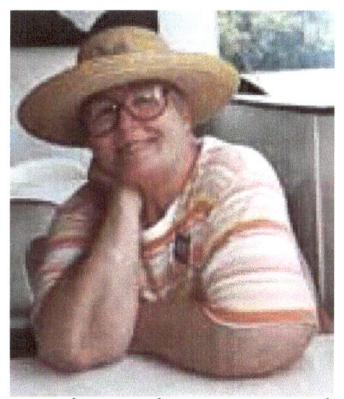

About the Author & Artist. Arlene Wright-Correll (1935- ___), popular American award winning Artist, author and avid gardener, at the age of 68, decided to pick up her paint brushes again after 54 years and paint, in mostly gouache watercolors and pastels, the flowers, herbs and fruits that grow at Home Farm Herbery in Munfordville, KY.

Though she paints in all mediums, she likes to use the Gouache paints, which are a heavy, opaque watercolor paint, sometimes called body color, producing a less wet-appearing and more strongly colored picture than ordinary watercolor. Occasionally, she will paint something from her world travels especially of Scotland, Ireland, or the Mediterranean. She is fond of those old memories. She is the resident artist and workshop instructor at Avalon Stained Glass Studio. She is also a **certified South Central KY Arts and Crafts Guild artist,** a **Certified EBSQ artist** and a **nominated member to The Museum of Women's Art** in Washington, DC. Ms. Wright-Correll is the creator and writer of **Who's Who in KY Arts and Crafts** and a member of **KAHT. Exhibitions:** Western KY University Celebration of the Arts, 2007 & South Central KY Cultural Center, Glasgow KY, 2007, Artist of the Month, Horse Cave Book Store, 2006, 1st place winner Salis International, Colorado Springs, May 2005. Hydras Watercolors. Her original paintings are sold quite quickly and one can always try and pick up whatever current one she is working on. The amazing thing about this "young" artist is that as a mother of 5 & the grandmother of 5, she is also a cancer and stroke survivor who is able to strive forward each and everyday to welcome the beauty of this small planet.

She is also a China & Porcelain painter, Stained Glass Artisan, Works in Fused Glass and Encaustic Art. She is one of the six KY Artists who worked 6 months to create the dolls for Journey Jots in 2006. Her favorite motto is a quote by Ruth Smelter., "You have not lived a perfect day, even though you have earned your money, unless you have done something for someone who cannot repay you."

"Tread the Earth lightly" and in the meantime.. May your day be filled with… **Peace, Light and Love,**

Arlene Wright-Correll

To see more of her work visit Avalon Stained Glass School, Studio & Art Gallery
100 Dave Wintsch Rd. Munfordville, KY 42765
Tuesday – Friday 9 to 5, Saturday 8 to noon
www.learn-america.com (270) 524 9567
Please check their site often. New paintings are being added all the time.
Or go to www.learn-america.com/stories/storyReader$158
Directions to studio: from Munfordville Courthouse go North on 357 for 2 miles, Right onto 2185 for 3..3 miles, Right onto Dave Wintsch Rd. and we are the 1st driveway on the left.

After working with artists and crafters for over a year since founding the South Central Arts and Crafts Guild in Munfordville, KY, I started to realize that our little county housed many talented people and I as talked to them I further realized that many people did not know they existed.

Along the way I discovered that this extended far beyond Hart County and that the state of Kentucky was filled with many, many talented people. Some people knew about, many were unknown. Some were professionals trying to make a living and many were amateurs trying to become professionals.

It became clear that there was a need for some type of medium to expose all this information to the public.

This generated the birth of **Who's Who in Kentucky Arts and Crafts**© which I started to publish it on the website, www.learn-america.com and which I place on the internet connecting via meta tags to places like Google. However, it needed another format, especially for our local artists and I went to Jobe Publishers and asked if they were interested in a column called **Who's Who in Kentucky Arts and Crafts**© and they were.

Every week I started to interview artists and craftsman around our town, county, nearby towns and across Kentucky. I was able to meet with many, many interesting and talented people.

It became quite clear that something else was coming out of this column, a forum where artists and crafters could network with each other, a place where information was shared and a place where the reader could learn more about some of the arts and crafts that the artists were creating.

This was my way of "paying forward" by making the public aware of "starving artists" as we often call ourselves. It was a way; hopefully, sales might be generated for these artists each time one of these weekly articles appeared.

So now I have come to the conclusion that each year I will arrange to have an annual **Who's Who in Kentucky Arts and Crafts**© yearbook published which artists, crafters and hopefully buyers of their wares can find them.

Should you wish to be included in any future **Who's Who in Kentucky Arts and Crafts**© just call me at (270) 524 9567 or email me at askarlene@scrtc.com and put **Who's Who in Kentucky Arts and Crafts**© in the subject line and I will get right back to you. Don't hide your light under a bushel basket. It's free. Let's get the word out!

Meet Kentucky artist Milena Soukal

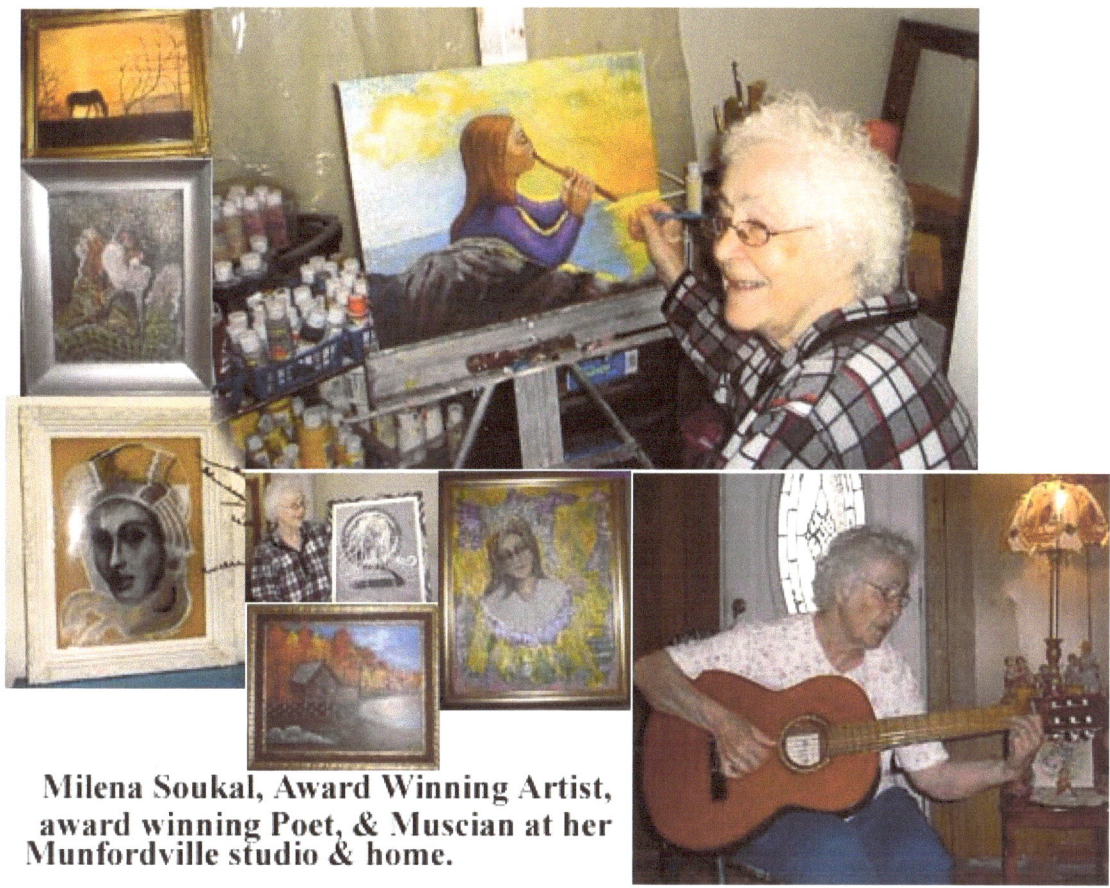

Milena Soukal, Award Winning Artist, award winning Poet, & Muscian at her Munfordville studio & home.

83 years ago Milena entered this world in Slovenia. She lived there with her mother, father, 2 sisters and her brother until the peace was disrupted with WWII. Milena was a grade school teacher who taught grades 1-12. As singers and musicians she and her two sisters had a successful radio show in Slovenia. Her life took a horrible turn when the powers to be (America, England & Russia) decided that Slovenia was to be turn over to the Communists in 1945.

Her family, being strong anti-communists, was in trouble. She and her siblings tried to convince her mother to escape with them to Austria. They failed, but her mother encouraged them to try it by themselves. Her two sisters left first, and then Milena and her brother fled together.

It was a terrible trek, under Russian gun fire and siege, no cars, just horses and carts, people and horses being shot all around them, they spent 3 days in a mountain pass, because the roads were jammed with thousands of escaping Germans, Serbs, Italians and all others fleeing the communists. They hid in a tunnel jammed with others fleeing to freedom. Chaos abounded, all languages mixed together.

They finally got into Austria, but not to freedom as we Americans know it. They were met by her two sisters and all were put into a refugee camp where Milena lived for 5 long years with thousands and thousands of other refugees. At first in a big field, no food, shelter, nothing. Eventually they organized themselves. They found canvas, made a tent; at first food was made from the dead horses and mules. It is here that she met her husband in this camp, they married, and two of her 4 children were born in that camp.

While in the camp, the Americans, English and Russian were being besieged by the Austrians to take these refugees. Finally the Russians agreed to take11, 000 anti-communists out of the camp and word got back to Milena that all 11,000 were shot to death!

At last the Slovenia League from America stepped in. Milena, her husband and 2 babies were some of the chosen to come to America. Penniless, they were transported to Germany where they waited 6 more weeks until they flown by the Army to New York. Here they were met by more people from the Slovenia League who gave them $5.00 in cash which Milena said they had to repay once they were working. Other people helped them with food, clothing and getting an apartment. Her husband got a job as a janitor. After 4 years, they moved to Chicago where he worked in a steel mill. Their family grew during this time, when 2 more sons were born. During their life in Chicago and as the boys grew older Milena began work at Sears Roebuck.

Milena and her husband worked hard, saved and eventually bought a home, they raised 4 fine sons, even were able to buy a small farm in Munfordville in 1985 as a summer place.

In 1978 & in 1980 her art won first place in one of Sears & Roebuck's art contests. An accomplished poet Milena also won several awards during the time she lived in Chicago. Milena is also a talented musician and singer.

Her husband died in 1989 and Milena decided she needed the peace and tranquility of Munfordville to continue her art work. Much to her 4 son's dismay she left the hustle and bustle of Chicago moved full time to their summer place in 1990.

An avid gardener, she maintains her place with the beauty that perseveres through all the travails she has endured. A few years ago, her 33 year old son was cutting down a tree for her when it fell on him and killed him adding another chilling and sad event for Milena.

Milena's artwork continues each day. She belongs to the South Central Kentucky Arts & Crafts Guild. When she is not painting, she is gardening, or crocheting many items she has for sale or gives to her grandchildren.

Meet Kentucky artist Donita Crain-Woodcock

Donita Crain-Woodcock grew up in Munfordville, Kentucky. Donita is a watercolorist, muralist, illustrator, crafts person, stained glass artisan and a musician who plays piano, flute, drums and is currently learning the bass guitar.

She says "She started her career as an artist early in life, doing murals on the walls of her bedroom with crayons. Much to her mother's dismay, and was guided to a more traditional "paper" support for her self-expression!"

Since then, with no formal training, Donita has explored every medium that she has had access to. It has just been in the last couple of years that she has seriously pursued painting in watercolor.

Having had a "Eureka" moment during instruction from Mary Lou Hall, and Nona Atkisson. It was like coming home. She had found her medium! Donita fell in love with the flow and brilliance that watercolors offer.

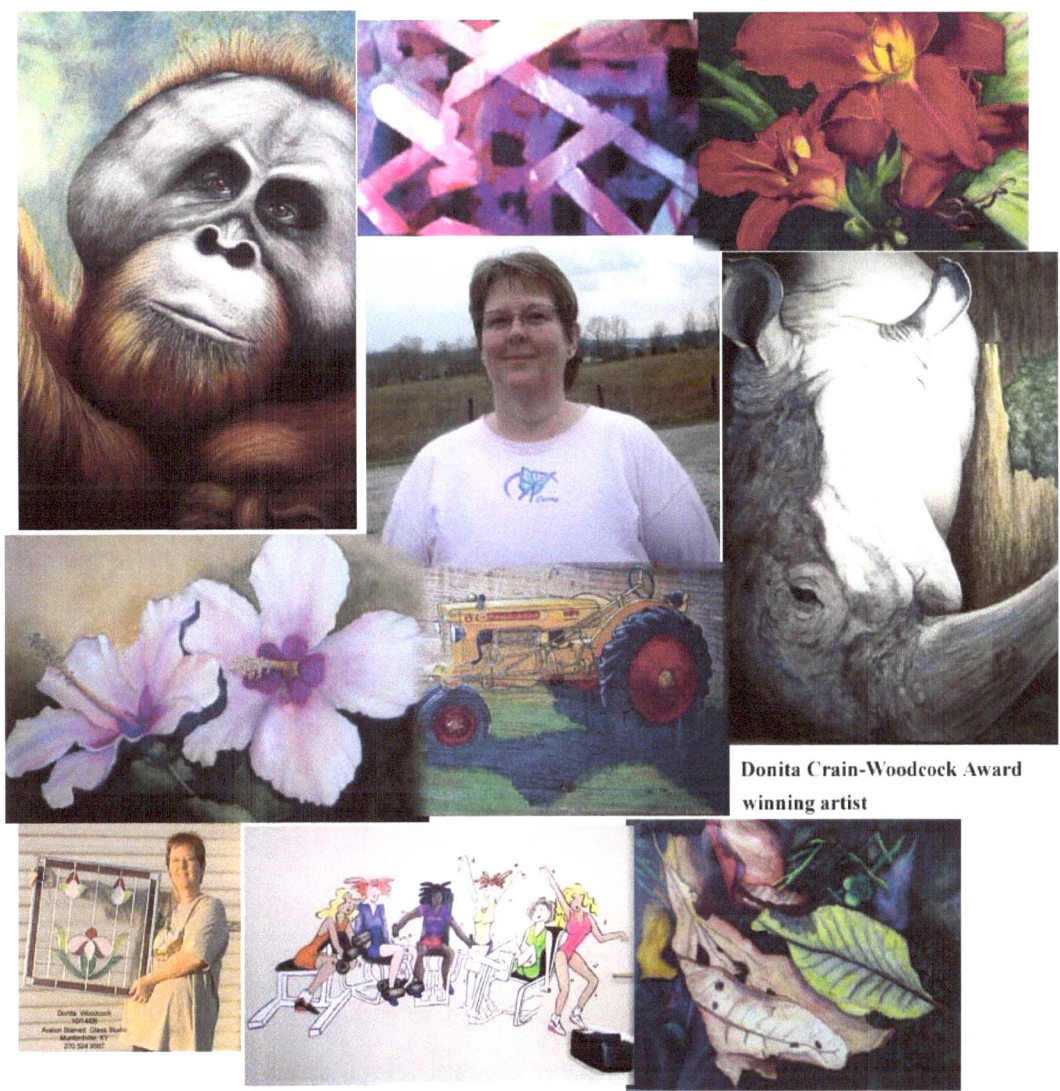

Donita Crain-Woodcock Award winning artist

In 2005 she won several honorable mentions in, realistic, art, collage, drawing and a third place at the Kentucky State Fair in transparent watercolor, upon her first time entering. In July and September of 2004 she was named artist of the month in Central Kentucky Arts Guild who meet once a month in Elizabethtown. This past December 2005 she was again named artist of the month.

Many of her subjects are close-ups of lone flowers or animals. In the singularity of her subjects she hopes to portray the wonder and awesome beauty of God's creation.

Locally, Donita's works have been on display at the State Theater, and other Elizabethtown Business exhibits such as Barnes and Noble, Cobblers Café & State Theater. She is a juried member of CKAG, formerly chairperson Artist of the Month program and currently serving as Vice President. She is also a member and treasurer of SCKA&CG.

Recently Donita discovered another talent at an Avalon Stained Glass Studio workshop and her first project was an incredible large panel. Since then she has added that to her artistic skills.

As a muralist in demand, Donita recently did the large mural in the Munfordville Curves.

Donita also teaches sketching; drawing and watercolor workshops and her work can be seen at Crain's Matting &Framing in Munfordville. She can be reached at 524 3548 or email her at rondon@scrtc.com for more information on either seeing her work or signing up for a class.

Donita says she would love to travel more and expand her art.

Recently Donita discovered another talent at an Avalon Stained Glass Studio workshop and her first project was an incredible large panel. Since then she has added that to her artistic skills.

As a muralist in demand, Donita recently did the large mural in the Munfordville Curves.

Donita also teaches sketching; drawing and watercolor workshops and her work can be seen at Crain's Matting &Framing in Munfordville. She can be reached at 524 3548 or email her at rondon@scrtc.com for more information on either seeing her work or signing up for a class.

Donita says she would love to travel more and expand her art.

Meet Kentucky artist Gary Reynolds of Craddock Rd. Munfordville, KY.

Gary Reynolds is native of Munfordville. He has worked at Louisville Bedding for 29 years and is a picker jack operator. He is also a wood carving artist.

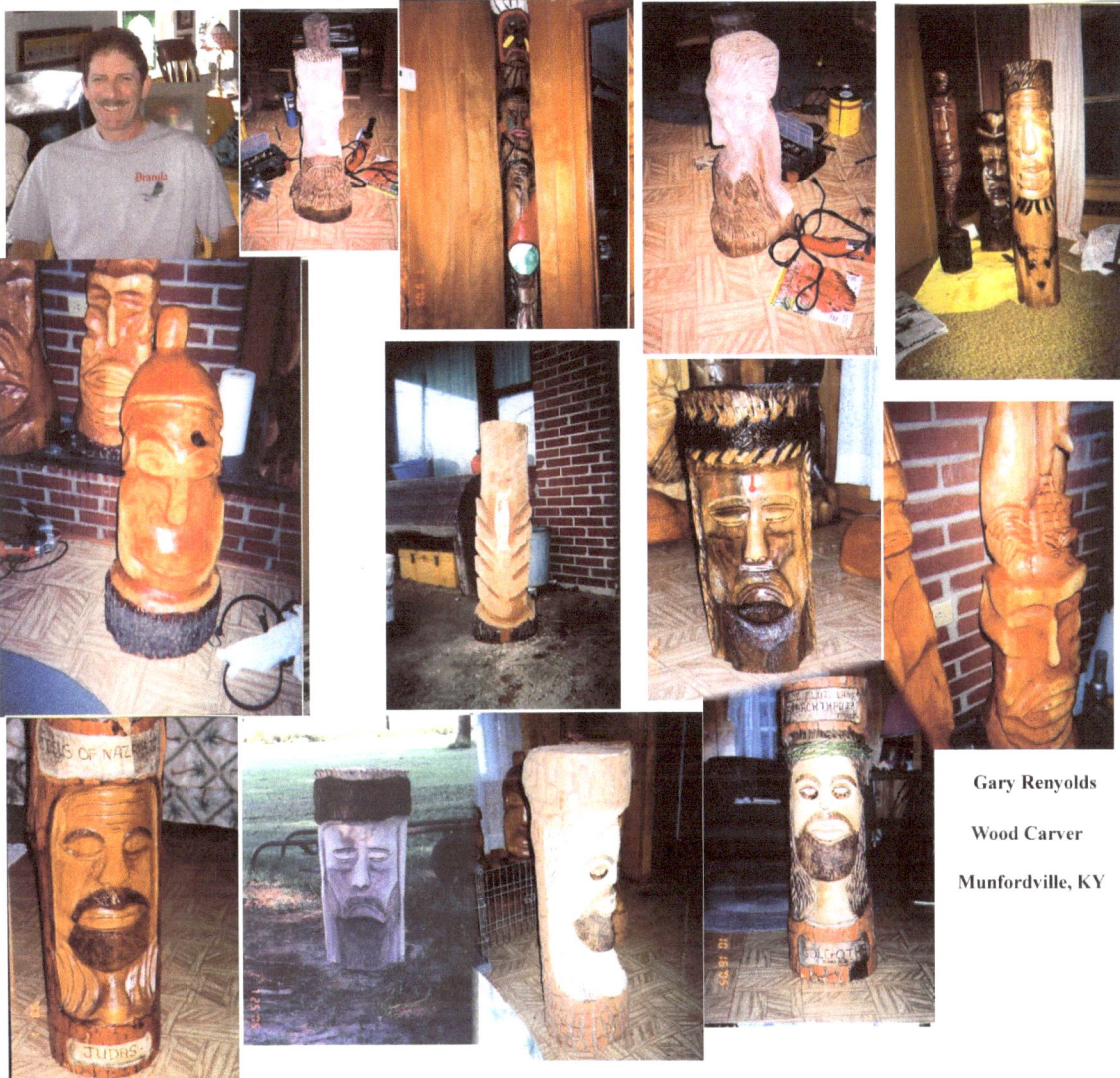

Gary Renyolds

Wood Carver

Munfordville, KY

About 15 years ago Gary started doing rough wood carving with a chain saw. His wood carving art continued to grow as he tested out different kinds of wood. His most favorite kind of wood is Sassafras. He favors walnut, white oak, red oak and pin oak. Over the years his experiments with cherry wood, proved nice grains, but even after seasoning, they tended to crack.

He spends a great deal of time tracking down the wood he feels is just what he is looking for and he finds it in many different places. Some times it is just one piece and some times it may be as many as 40 pieces. Often the wood is quite a distance from his home studio and then he has to haul it home, store it so it dries and seasons. There is a lot of time put into each piece before Gary even takes the chain saw to it.

This is not a light weight hobby as Gary says most pieces weigh at least 100 pounds. Two years ago Gary started to refine his wood carving art with the use of grinders, dremels and drills. This allowed him to put finer features on his work.

He has created over 50 pieces of art wood carvings and some reside in different parts of Kentucky and in Indiana. His work is reasonably priced and starts at $200.00. He has a lot of them for display at his home and he can be reached at 524 7952 for a viewing appointment.

Gary says it takes about a weekend of carving just to rough cut out a piece and then the time to take his finishing tools to it until he is satisfied with it. Once he feels the piece is completed he then puts a natural stain on it and polyurethane.

He gets great satisfaction from this and says the beauty of his wood carving art is in the eye of the beholder, just as it is with any artist's finished creation. Gary is also a lover and collector of art and wood carving and often buys other wood carver's creative pieces or other artist paintings.

He is constantly expanding his knowledge about his craft and recently discovered and joined the South Central Kentucky Arts and Crafts Guild.

Meet Kentucky artist Gordon Cottrell of Bonnieville, KY

Gordon Cottrell, a native of Kentucky, worked at Dow Corning in Elizabethtown until retiring in the late 90's. During that time, Gordon felt he needed a hobby and he is the first to admit he is not a carpenter or a mechanic, but he had a good hand for sketching and drawing. So in 1959 he started his hobby in art.

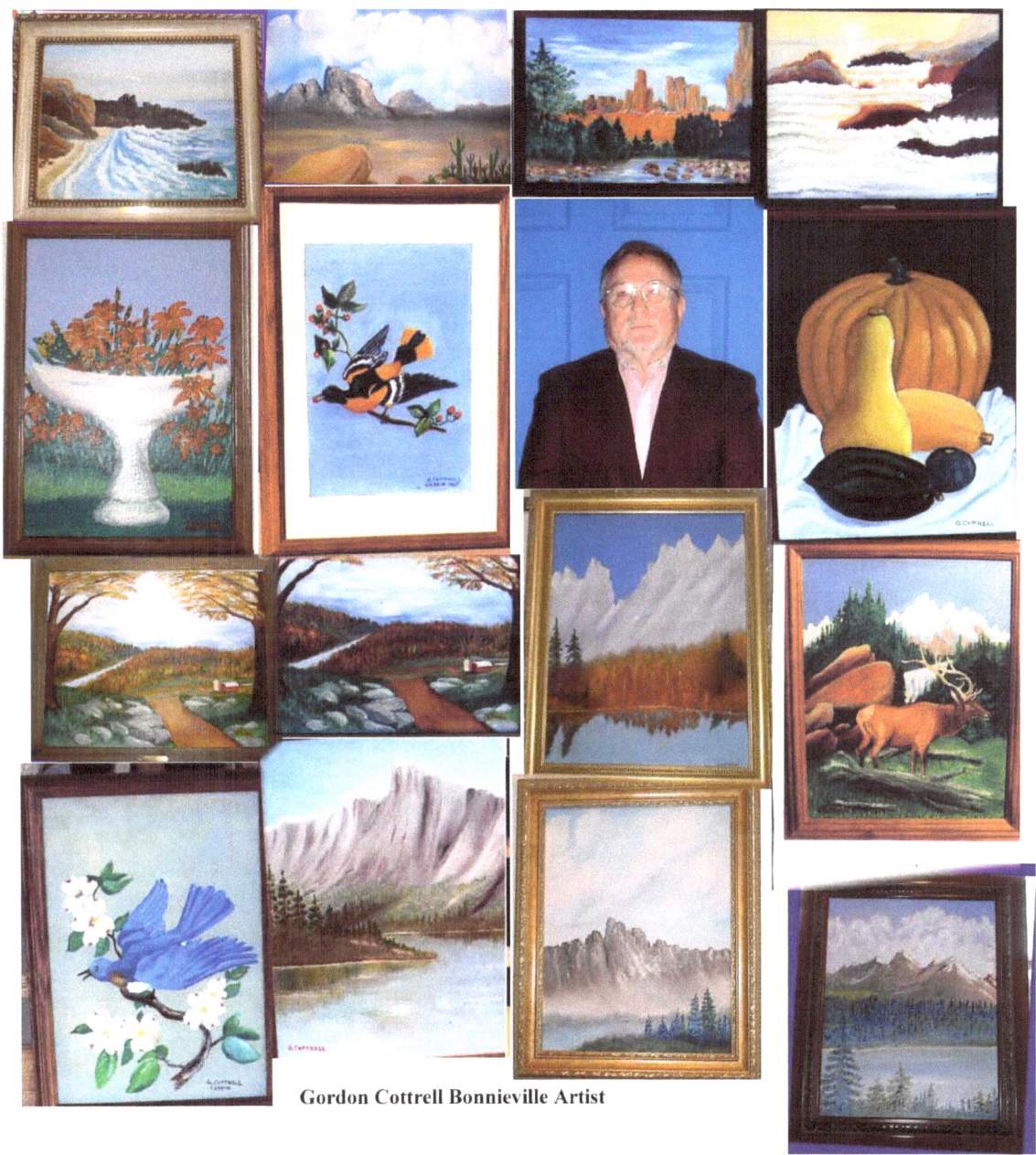

Gordon Cottrell Bonnieville Artist

He is a self-taught oil painter who did a lot of research into the Old Master and especially Frederick Taube's books. This artist inspired Gordon to investigate the techniques of this style of painting.

Gordon started out in Tempera which uses 3 parts egg yolk, 1 & ½ part water, 1 part stand oil & 1 part Copal Varnish with the ground paint pigments. Then he graduated to casein which uses bee's wax mixed with casein and paint pigments. About 1969 or 70, Gordon moved on to oil painting.

Gordon feels that painting is like building a building; one has to lay a good foundation and build the painting from there.

During his time as a hobbyist artist he painted many fine paintings and they hang in many peoples homes. He gave them as gifts or they just paid for the materials. After retiring, Gordon decided to become a serious artist and hopefully to get his work to pay for itself.

Now Gordon feels he is good enough to enter his paintings into National Art Contests and he says though he has not won anything yet, at least his paintings pass the arduous test of being accepted. He has started to do commission work in both landscapes and portraits and his work can be viewed by appointment only or for setting up a commission by calling 270 531 3022.

Last year he built himself an art studio in his home. Gordon's wife Linda is his most ardent supporter and fan. He says he is getting serious and paints more than ever before, except when the fishing bug hits him. Then he takes his sketch pad and pencils to get ideas for his paintings.

In 2005 Gordon & his wife Linda joined the South Central Kentucky Arts & Crafts Guild and Linda was elected Vice President of the Guild.

Meet Kentucky artist Jef Dirig of Glasgow, KY

Serendipity plays a large part in our lives and that proved true the other day when I was over in Bowling Green, KY in the framing section of Hobby Lobby. I passed by a young man with a series of beautiful paintings that lay out to be framed.

Did you paint those I asked? "Yes", said a young man named Jeffrey Dirig. We introduced ourselves to each other and I learned that this artist had moved to Glasgow 3 years ago. He lives there with his wife, who is a doctor at T.J. Sampson and their two small sons Joshua and Jacob. Dirig has an undergraduate degree in Medical Illustration.

In 2002 he was nationally juried by Robert Bateman and along with about 70 other artists attended the Bear Tooth School of Art in Montana and studied with the recently deceased famous artist Paco Young. He is modest about another one of his achievements for receiving an International award on a collegiate level for a text book on equestrian medical illustrations.

Jef, as he signs his work, aside from helping out with Joshua and Jacob, devotes his full time as an artist at his Lake Ridge Studio in Glasgow. He says, "He considers himself to be a "Back Road" artist".

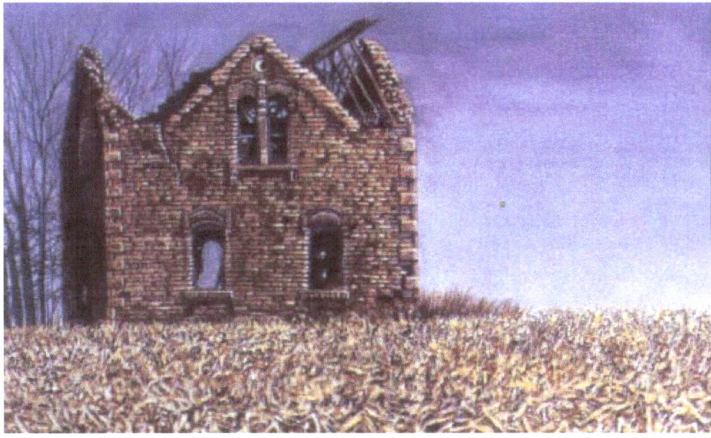 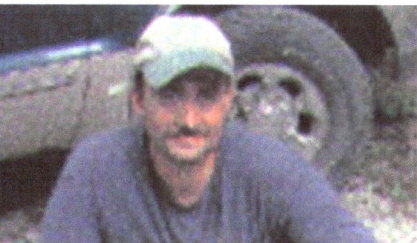

Jef Dirig with one of his lovely Paintings. Lake Ridge Studio 150 Lake Ridge Rd. Glasgow, KY 270 646 4196

His beautiful work is done with a watercolor technique using egg yolks. Jef says, "Living on the edge of the Appalachian mountain range has provided a lifetime supply of subject matter." He finds many subjects for his art on and around the pristine lakes of the area. With the rivers dammed and the valleys flooded years ago, it changed the road structure forever and left countess areas where time seems to have stopped. Ruined buildings, abandoned vehicles, old farm equipment are just some of the things Jef paints as he brings them back to life. Jef says," The Japanese have a term for this kind of beauty, called Wabi Sabi, which basically means having an appreciation for naturally occurring imperfections."

His artist eye is the camera to bring to life the memories of America's forgotten back roads. It leads us to think about a time when nature flourished in abundance and people were more self-reliant. Gazing at his pictures takes one into a frozen window of time long since past.

His paintings portray local landscapes that oft times include wildlife or man-made objects that have been worn by time. Dirig also refers to himself as a folk artist although his painting style is very refined. He begins his painting by drawing a detailed black and white sketch to establish the composition and contrast. Once he is completely satisfied with the layout of the objects and the details, it is only then that he sets up his canvas. "It will take me from one day to several months to finish the piece," he says, "depending upon the size of the painting and how well things are going." When things don't go well, Jef says, "The piece usually winds up on the burn pile." Obviously these 3 paintings did not wind up in the burn pile.

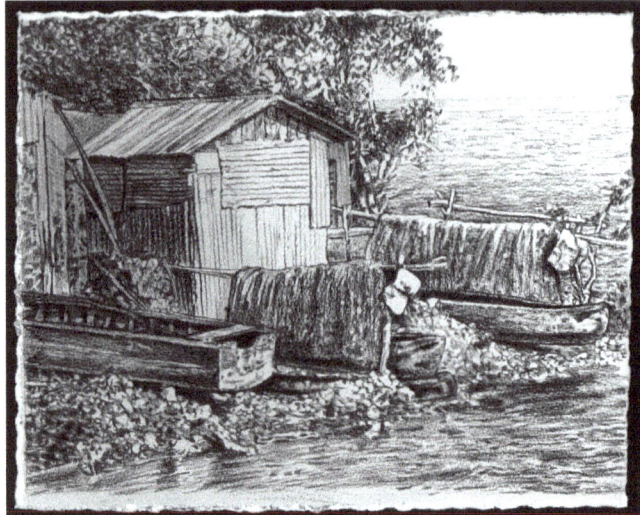

Notice the Bobcat in the painting to the right.

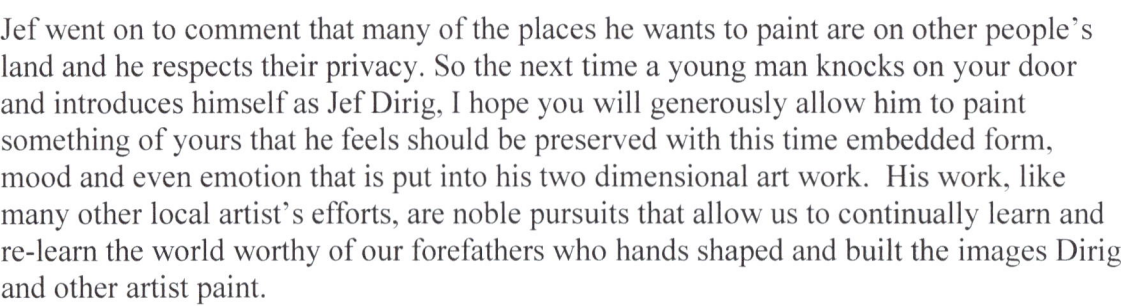

Jef went on to comment that many of the places he wants to paint are on other people's land and he respects their privacy. So the next time a young man knocks on your door and introduces himself as Jef Dirig, I hope you will generously allow him to paint something of yours that he feels should be preserved with this time embedded form, mood and even emotion that is put into his two dimensional art work. His work, like many other local artist's efforts, are noble pursuits that allow us to continually learn and re-learn the world worthy of our forefathers who hands shaped and built the images Dirig and other artist paint.

During our conversation we got around to art reproductions in the form of Giclee prints, pronounce Gee-Clay. Jef has just purchased all the equipment to reproduce his art in this form and he will be offering this service to other local artists. This is a big boon to the artists of this area as the closest similar services are way over in Louisville and that means doing a lot of driving back and forth to check the proofs or dealing with a company on the internet.

All of his work is for sale and to see Jef Dirig's beautiful paintings or to have your own art reproduced into Giclee prints go to Lake Ridge Studio at 150 Lake Ridge Rd., Glasgow, KY 42141 or call for an appointment 270 646 4196

Meet Kentucky artist Harriet Crain

Harriet Crain, a native of Franklin, TN, moved to Munfordville, KY in 1954 and lives on Lonoke Rd. with her husband Randall. A few houses down from their home, Harriet has her art studio in the same building that houses Crain's Matting and Framing and a small gift shop filled with original KY arts and crafts created by Harriet and her two artistic daughters who also live nearby.

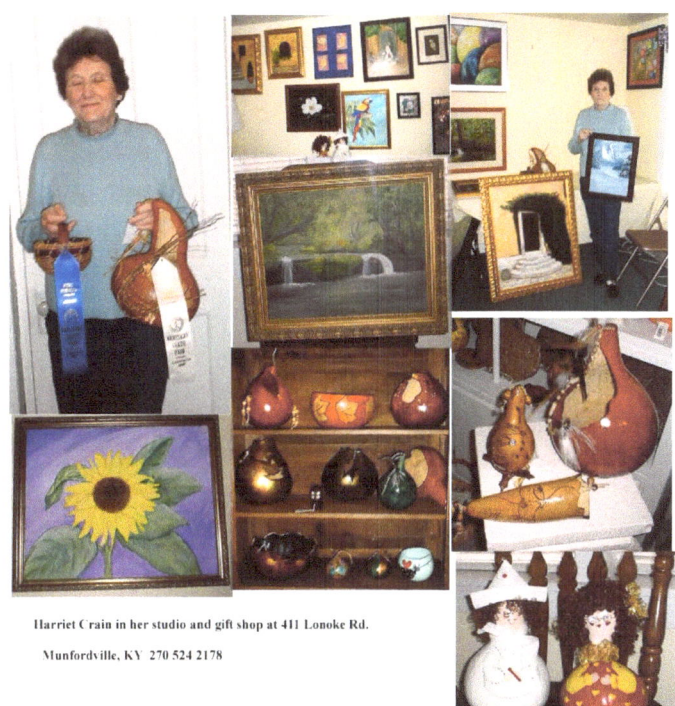

15 years ago Harriet was inspired by a display of hand painted gourds she saw at a craft show in TN. She thought she would try her hand at this. Though Harriet no longer raises her own gourds, she did in the early years. She enjoyed this folk craft and it developed over the years into a spectacular display of gourd products.

Harriet Crain in her studio and gift shop at 411 Lonoke Rd. Munfordville, KY 270 524 2178

She learned all kinds of techniques and was creating gourd people, gourd birdhouses, gourd pitchers, gourd bird feeders, gourd baskets and just about anything you can think of including gourd jewelry. Her gourd people are delightful. Need a nurse, policeman, school teacher, snow man, Halloween decorations or other holiday decorations or people? Harriet is the lady to see as she takes special orders to create a unique gourd person just for you.

Harriet now buys her gourds, but it still takes a curing and drying process of approximately 5 months to get them ready to work on. Her techniques not only include painting the gourds, but also she does carvings and wood burning designs, such as an Indian motif, on them. Amazingly some of her gourds look and feels like wood when she is finished. This technique involves a leather stain and when she wants them shiny she uses a polyurethane finish on them thus making them look and feel like wood. Other times she just uses a matte finish. She also does floral arrangements with her gourds.

Often she weaves some basket material into the gourds and in 2004 one such gourd basket of hers won 1st place at the Kentucky State Fair. She also uses braiding, beads and feathers on her gourds making them truly artistic and unique. One of her gourds took 3rd place in the fine arts and crafts section of the 2004 Kentucky State Fair which was quite an accomplishment since there was an amazing and complex assortment of artistic endeavors competing against her. Harriet is a member of the Kentucky Gourds Society.

About 3 years ago she overheard some ladies in the Bowling Green Hobby Lobby shop talking about an on-going free painting workshop that meets every Tuesday at the 1st Christen Church in Elizabethtown. These ladies were kind enough to give her more information and invited her to visit the workshop. Harriet has been going there practically every Tuesday for the past 3 years. She says it is a wonderful workshop full of information, inspiration and fellowship and it is free. It has lead her to become an active painter in oils and acrylics.

This led her to join the South Central Kentucky Art Guild and 2 years ago 3 of her paintings were juried, thus allowing her to enter her art in business places and galleries. She paints in oils and acrylics and she has had her work hung in shows in the First Federal Bank in Elizabethtown, Celia Bank in Elizabethtown, the Cobbler Café and the State Theater, also in Elizabethtown.

In 2004 Harriet attended a Robert Hoffman plein air workshop, thus furthering her skills and art techniques.

In March of 2004 she was instrumental in helping to form the South Central Kentucky Arts & Crafts Guild. Harriet is the current president of SCKA&CG.

Her work can be seen and purchased at Crain's Matting and Framing at 411 Lonoke Rd., (Rte 571) Munfordville or viewed by appointment by calling 270 524 2178

Meet Kentucky artist Randall Crain.

We tend to forget that framing in itself is an art. No artist's painting; photo or print is complete without a good matting and frame to enhance it.

Framing and matting is expensive even when craft places offer 50% off sales. However, right here in Munfordville, we have a master framer and matting specialist named Randall Crain.

Randall, a native of Hardin County was born on a farm in Sonora and moved to Munfordville when he was 15.

One of his hobbies was woodworking and upon retiring as a computer info systems specialist at Lord Corp. in Bowling Green, Randall unwittingly moved in framing.

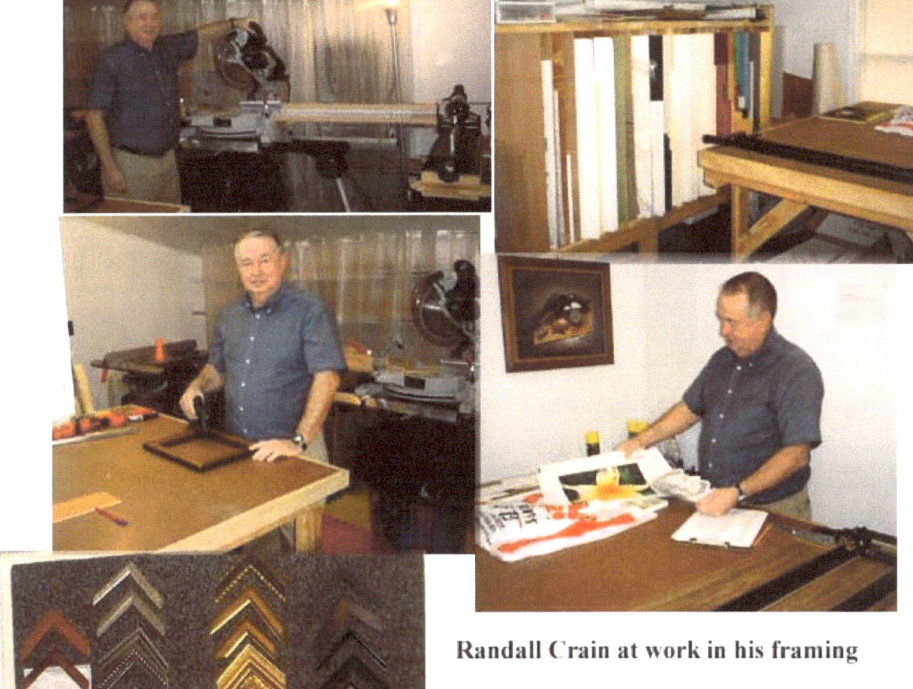

Randall Crain at work in his framing Studio at 411 Lonoke Rd. in Munfordville, KY

His nephew required picture frames for his art, His artistic cousin also and gave Randall a professional mat cutter. Having an award winning artist as a wife and two daughters as artists further pushed Randall into becoming a professional framer after he retired.

He has since acquired all the professional tools of the trade. His fame as a gifted framer has spread outside the county and artists from other counties drive over and bring Randall their work simply because he does a great job at a really affordable price.

17

He frames photos, oil paintings, watercolors, pastels, and just about anything. He has a great variety of matting stock and frames to choose from. Randall says, "Framing the work of pastelists is one of the hardest jobs, as it has to be framed with picture grade acrylic.

Randall's finished products are all ready to be professionally juried since he knows that an artist may want to enter a piece later on into a showing or contest.

His artist wife, Harriet says, "Randall is a perfectionist, taking about 2 hours to frame each piece regardless of the size, simply because he will not let a picture leave the studio without it being done to his ultimate satisfaction". "He is his own greatest critic," his daughters say.

Randall has done mirrors, shadow boxes and he does a lot of framing for the Louisville Watercolor Society since his work is up to their standards for professional showing.

Do you have a favorite frame and picture? Just bring it to Randall and he will help you choose the right matting and you will have a lovely piece when he is done and at a very affordable price. He does single matting, double, triple, you name it. He is able to shadow box frame your most precious memento or eclectic art work.

Randall says, "This work is really gratifying and I enjoy what I do. I have a nice little studio shop (Crain's Matting and Framing) at 411 Lonoke Rd. (Rte 571) in Munfordville, KY. My overhead is low, so my prices are really affordable. I don't keep regular store hours since I live just up the road from it and when anyone wants something framed, they just call me at 270 524 2178, tell me when they are coming and I meet them there. When the work is done, I call them and they come and pick it up. It works out well for both of us. With 3 artists in the family and being a member of the South Central Kentucky Arts & Crafts Guild, I keep fairly busy, yet I welcome and always find time to make room for a new customer or artist."

Meet Kentucky artist Theresa Shelton

Growing up on a small farm in Hardin County, KY gave Theresa Shelton the time to nurture her artistic abilities at an early age. Many of her subjects reflect a passion for this rural life.

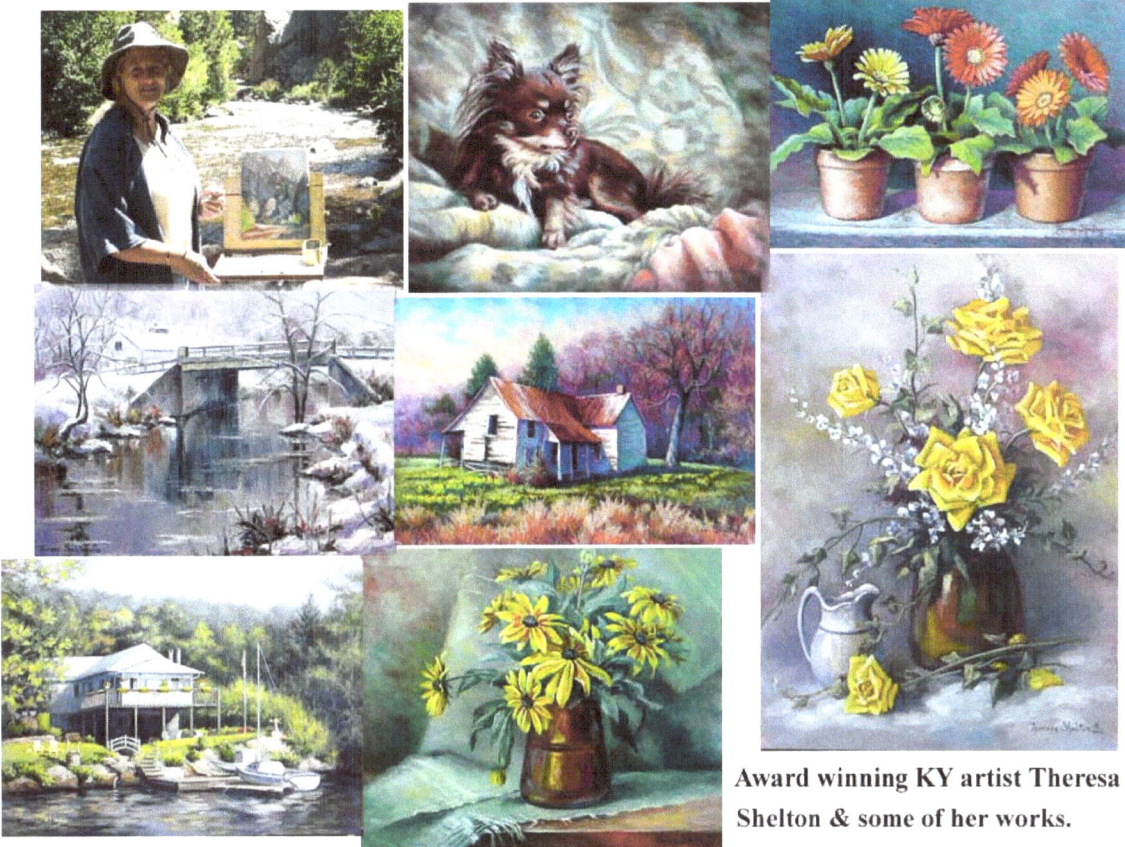

Award winning KY artist Theresa Shelton & some of her works.

Theresa was lucky to have a mother who observed a creative side to her daughter and she was encouraged at every opportunity. Theresa says, *"At the age of 10, I received a Jon Gnaggy drawing set for Christmas and faithfully copied every exercise."* So began a life long dream to become an artist. Self taught during her early years, Theresa has expanded her techniques by studying under such renowned artist as Cheng Khee Chee, Gerald Brommer, Robert Hoffman, Dean Davis and Charles Gruppe.

Through the years, Theresa has not moved far from her roots. She married Tim Shelton in 1978 and six months later they purchased Haynes Greenhouse in Vine Grove, KY where they have enjoyed working together for the past 26 years. The greenhouse gave Theresa an outlet for her creativity and subject matter for her paintings.

Looking at her art, the viewer will see that she finds pleasure in creating pieces that are tranquil and soothing to the eye. Working in a realist style, her favorite mediums are oil and pastel. She regularly spends time painting 'en plein aire', depicting scenes from her hometown and the surrounding area. Working on location gives her a personal connection with the subject. Even when the final piece is created in the studio, the experience of being up close and personal with the subject adds emotion to her paintings.

A founding member and past president of the Central Kentucky Art Guild, Theresa finds inspiration and growth by surrounding herself with other artists. Members of the Central Kentucky Art Guild voted Ms. Shelton 'Artist of the Year' for 2001. She is also an 'Exhibiting Member' of the Kentucky Guild of Artists and Craftsmen, a juried participant in Kentucky Crafted, 'The Market' and a juried member of Oil Painters of America.

Winning several awards in juried shows, her paintings hang in public and private collections throughout the United States and abroad.

Question, "What was the first medium you worked in?"
Answer, "When I started painting in the early 70's, the first medium I attempted was oils and to this day it is still my favorite. There is something exhilarating about working with all that soft mixable paint. I love to work wet-in-wet, letting each new brush stoke blend into the last. Through the years I have modified my approach, going from very realistic to a little more impressionistic. As an artist, I feel my technique is a work in progress, always trying to improve. Stagnation is not inspiring. Working from real life is my preferred method."

Question, "How do you feel about painting on location?"
Answer, "Going out on location to paint is such a learning experience compared to working in the studio. This past summer I took a trip with 3 other artists to Colorado for a week. I packed up my little pochade box with water mixable oils and stood out in the mountains painting. It was great."

Question, "Do you use photos prior to painting?"
Answer, "I always take photos of the places that interest me for reference to use once I get back to the studio, but I have my memories of being there to help interpret the scene. A painting shouldn't be just a copy of a photo; I strive to paint my feelings into them. In summer, I stroll through the farmer's market in search for fruit and flea markets for interesting objects to use in still life setups. That gives me actual forms to paint instead of using photos."

Question, "Do you work in other mediums other than oil paints?"
Answer, "I also work in watercolors and acrylics, but the most recent addition to my painting tools is soft pastels. I find they work similar to oils, but I get a sense of drawing when working with them. They have quickly become my second favorite medium. They are more immediate, with no mixing or any brushes to cleanup. They just sit there on the table waiting for me to have a few minutes to amuse myself with their multitude of colors. When I get involved in a painting, I loose track of time and forget all else around me." Theresa says, "Creating is something I have to do! It's part of who I am."

You can see Theresa's work by contacting her at *270-877-5853* to make an appointment to visit her studio at *645 Highland Ave.   Vine Grove, KY 40175 or email her at* tsstudio@theresashelton.com   more of her art work may be viewed by going to her website. www.theresashelton.com

Meet Kentucky artist Jan Stoller

Jan Stoller is a native of Glasgow, Ky. She married and moved to South Dakota and resided there for 10 years with her air force husband. After spending 30 years in Illinois she moved back to Cave City in 2003 with her elderly mother, her sister Joan Newell, (who is also a stained glass artist and art photographer, and their 2 life long friends.

They all live on The Lavender Hill Alpaca Farm where they professionally raise alpacas and "fainting" goats on their 28 acre farm which also sustains horses, various dogs and cats. You can visit their website http://www.lavenderhillalpacas.com/ to see all that is going on at this charming and friendly place.

Jan is a multi-talented artist swinging back and forth from 2 dimensional arts to 3 dimensional arts as the inspiration comes to her. Ten years ago she zeroed in on water color painting after spending some time working in oils.

After "The Lavender Hill Mob" as I call the girls, started up their Alpaca farm, Jan discovered she could take the Alpaca fiber and work with a craft called "needle felting".

Needle (or punch) felting is a process originally developed for making industrial felt. Large beds of steel needles are moved in and out of the loose fiber to create large sheets of felt. The felt needle has rough, notched edges that force the fiber down causing it to entangle with other fibers and create felt. Modern day felt artists have recently adopted the felt needle as a tool for creating dry felt and for use in conjunction with wet felting techniques. By using the needle individually, or in small clusters, felt artists can create very controlled designs and three-dimensional shapes that are difficult to achieve using traditional wet felt making techniques alone.

Jan works on a foam block and jabs her needle into the alpaca fiber, continually rolling the fiber and building up her creation until it resembles a teddy bear, a goat, or whatever she wants it to be. Jan starts with fairly deep jabs to make sure she is entangling the inner fibers. She says, "Both the angle and the depth of the jab are important for shaping. The fibers will go exactly where I put them. If I jab at an angle, the fibers go sideways. If I jab shallow, just the surface fibers are felted, creating a firm skin and a soft interior. When I jab deeply I can form deep indentations like arm and leg joints, eye sockets, waistlines, etc. If I jab at an angle, I have to be sure to keep the needle straight as it is very brittle and will break easily with very little sideways pressure. This requires a lot of poking!"

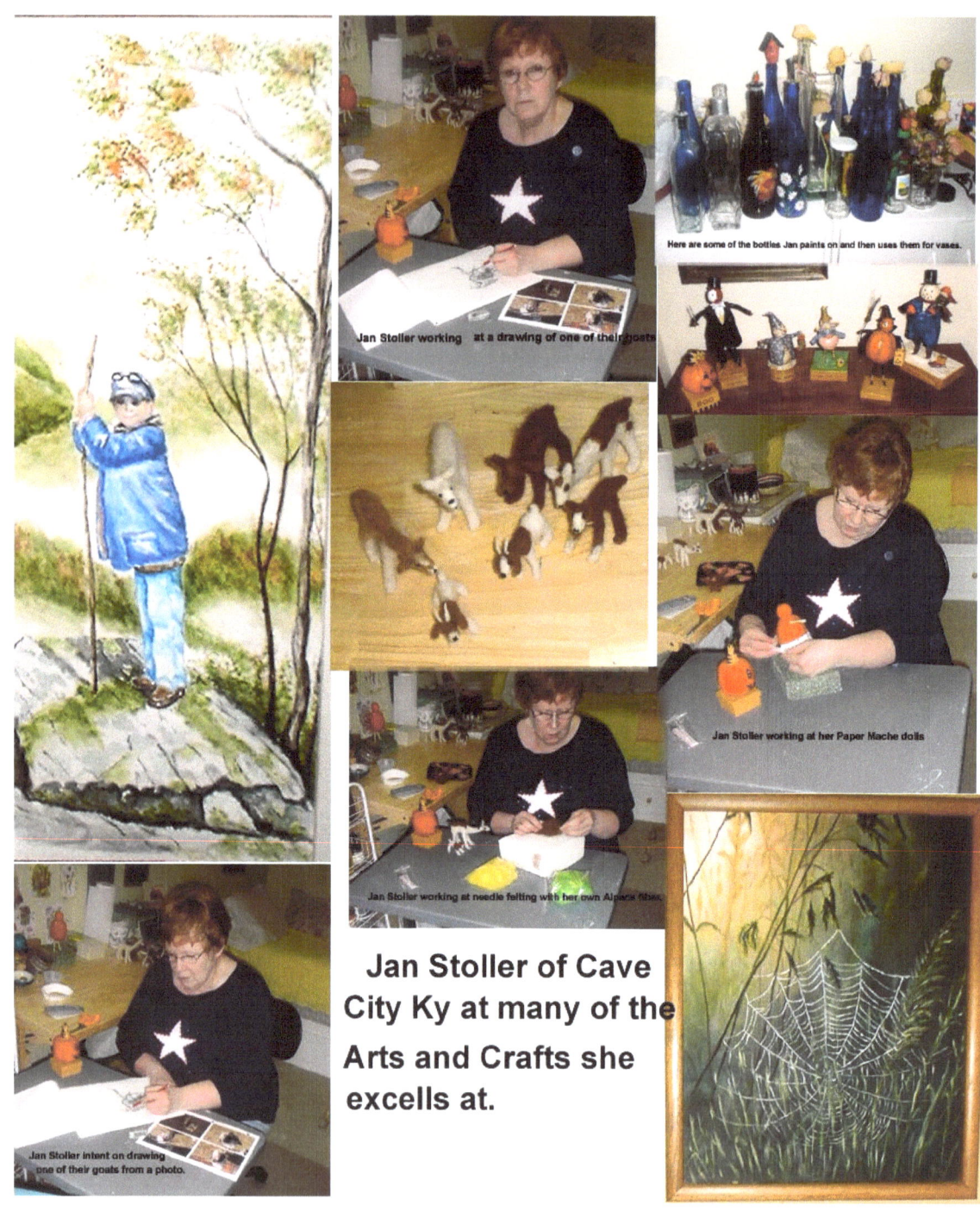

Here are some of the bottles Jan paints on and then uses them for vases.

Jan Stoller working at a drawing of one of their goats

Jan Stoller working at her Paper Mache dolls

Jan Stoller working at needle felting with her own Alpaca fibers.

Jan Stoller of Cave City Ky at many of the Arts and Crafts she excells at.

Jan Stoller intent on drawing one of their goats from a photo.

Jan colors the fiber with Kool Aid as it is the best colorant there is. She and her sister Joan have been saving up their Alpaca fibers and will be sending it off to get carded and spun into yarn which they will sell in their newest upcoming venture.

Currently they are working on a building they own in Cave City to develop a new business called, "The Cream and Sugar Café" where they will be serving breakfast and lunch. One can rely on it being good food, because both of them are excellent cooks!

As if she did not have enough to do, earlier this year Jan starting making the most incredible figures out of Paper Mache. When they are completed, she then paints them. These are truly artistic pieces which have a life of their own and the prices start at $200.00. Jan says, "Of all the things I do I find I like working with Paper Mache the best. It allows for totally creativity which emerges as I work with my supplies and the best thing is that it does not call for any special supplies from the craft store." Sounds easy enough, but until you have seen what Jan creates, it is far from easy. These are true works of art as far as this writer is concerned.

In amongst all these activities, Jan finds time to create lovely works of art by painting scenes or characters on colored glass bottles. I especially loved her polar bear painting on a lovely blue bottle.

Jan is always working on a project of some kind besides working at Caverna Florist. She has just finished up a water color painting of her grandson. Her studio is set up to handle all these artist endeavors and she flourishes at what she does.

Jan is an active member of the South Central Kentucky Arts and Crafts Guild and earlier this year she gave a demonstration of both needle felting and the Paper Mache people she makes to all the members of the South Central Kentucky Arts and Crafts Guild.

Her work will be for sale at "The Cream and Sugar Café" which will open summer of 2007 in Cave City, KY.

Meet Kentucky artists Ryan and Mary Pollard

 Often when one thinks of arts and crafts one does not think to include photography in those categories. However, not only is it an art, but taking a good photograph is an art in itself and one needs to be a craftsman to do it well. That person is Ryan Pollard, a Munfordville teen who is starting to really shine in this field.

His mom, Mary Pollard is a crafter who along with his dad saw this potential in Ryan. Together Ryan and Mary are a dynamic duo when it comes to putting arts and crafts together.

Mary a native of Minnesota moved to Munfordville with her husband Ken and their 2 sons in 1995. Mary has a lovely separate studio on their property to do all her crafts and her sewing as she is an excellent seamstress. She said Ken built it because he could not stand all her stuff all around the house.

Fifteen year old Ryan started taking photos when he was in the 4-H. He entered the "sequence of 3" exhibit with his blue bird photos and he won 3 Blue Ribbons in Photography at the 2005 KY State Fair. Ryan uses a Pentax digital 5 mega pixel camera.

After the KY State Fair Mary and Ryan decided they wanted to share his photos with others and they hit upon the idea of producing note cards and key chains.

Currently Ryan's photos are capturing the living history of Kentucky and especially Hart County. These tremendous keepsakes are tomorrow's archives of how life in KY is and was. Soon many of these old buildings will be gone and the artists of this area, including Ryan are keeping it alive with their paintings and photos.

Ryan and Mary have a new series coming up called "KY Tobacco Barns" and the photos besides being on key chains and note cards will be reproduced on pillows, tote bags and other things. These will soon be displayed at the Antique Mall in Glendale, KY.

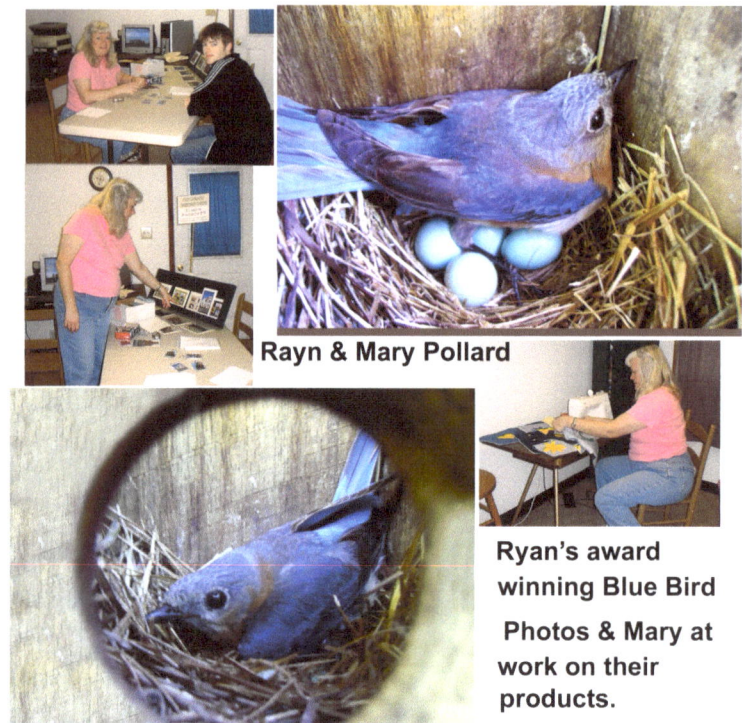

Rayn & Mary Pollard

Ryan's award winning Blue Bird Photos & Mary at work on their products.

Also in the works is a "Coca Cola photo series" consisting of photos of old KY buildings with the Coca Cola signs painted on them.

Ryan's photos are starting to gain fame as he looks for contests to enter and with Mary's contribution of adding them to crafts you soon will see them everywhere. Ryan's photos are copyrighted. Mary says, "All ready people are calling up to buy copies of Ryan's historical photos.

Mary is a current member of the South Central Kentucky Arts and Crafts Guild. Mary says, "One of my new projects will be to create art with quilt designs."

Mary and Ryan offer their KY historical note cards and key chains at wholesale prices to stores or shops who want to buy in bulk.

They currently sell their products retail from their home studio at 506 Boyd's Knob Rd. in Munfordville, KY and one can see all their crafts by calling for an appointment at 270 528 2462. You may also see their products by stopping in at the Hart County Historical Museum in Munfordville, KY

Meet Kentucky artist Carol Reesor

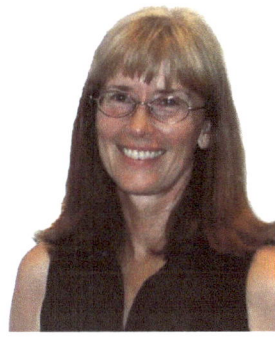

Carol Reesor was born in Elizabethtown, KY and currently lives in Buffalo, KY. I met Carol in April of 2005 where she and I were two of the 8 judges at a Congressional art show in Elizabethtown. I was impressed with her business cards which consisted of copies of her art work.

This year at Kentucky Market in Louisville I had the pleasure of seeing her work up close and was stunned by the beauty of her paintings. Carol has been painting since she became serious about it in 1974.

Her rural Kentucky studio provides a comfortable and fitting backdrop for her characteristically peaceful landscapes and engaging still-life compositions. Because it's important to Carol to capture a subject's essence, along with the natural effects of color and light, much of her landscapes are created on location or done from field studies. Carol says, "Growing up on a small farm gives me a connection with the land. When I see a beautiful scene I feel compelled to paint it." As a result, her work reveals an

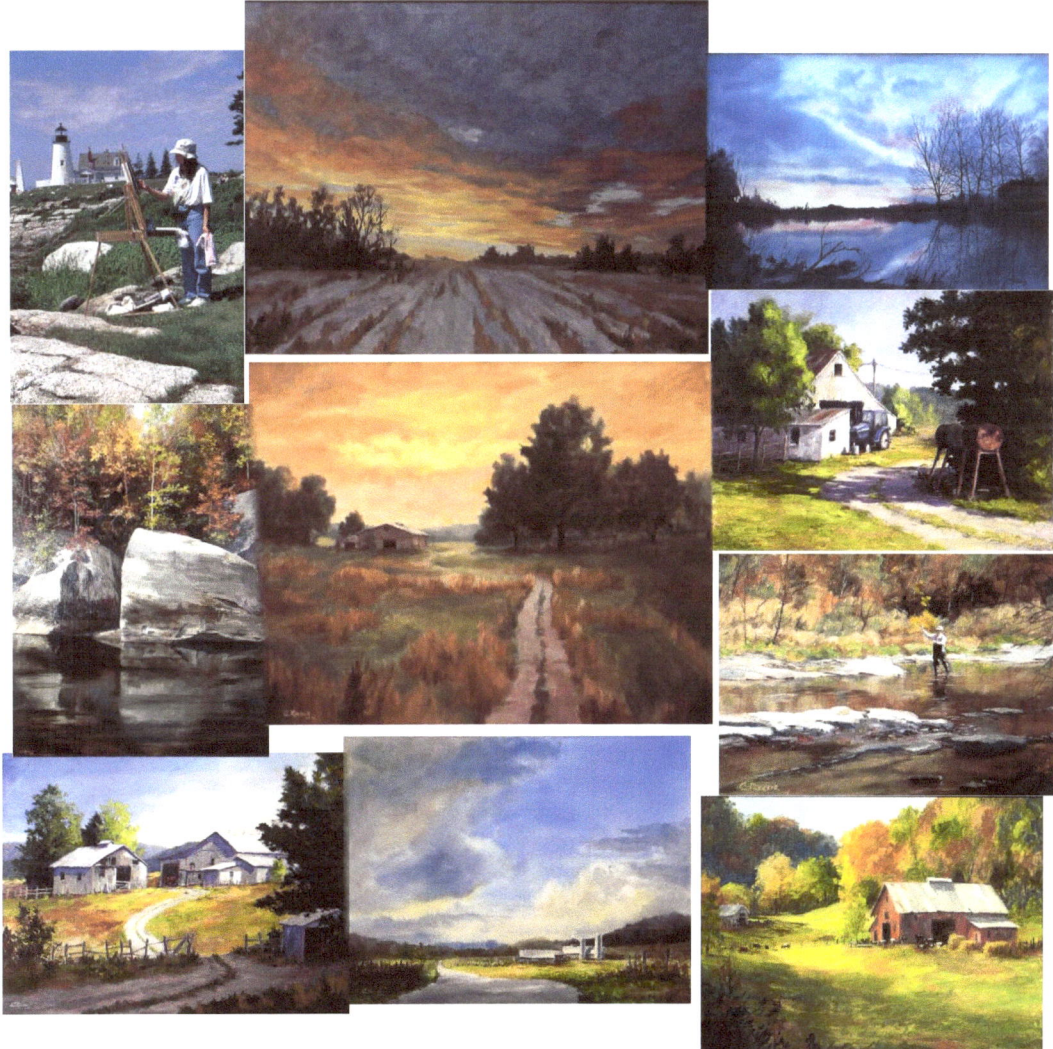

unpretentious truth that allows the viewer a sense of belonging to the scene and owning that moment in time.

She has an undeniable natural ability after years of developing and honing her skills, plus a passion for painting have all contributed to her well-developed style and notable success with her work. Carol says, "Watching an older sister sketch horses sparked her early interest and curiosity in developing her talent." A natural progression ensued. Drawing developed into oil painting and then watercolors.

Carol says she is always anxious to learn new things and over the past decade Carol has studied oil and watercolor techniques with several nationally known artists, including Robert Hoffman, Gerald Brommer, Dean Davis, Cheng Khee Chee, Joseph Fettingis, and Charles Gruppe.

Painting in both oils and watercolors, she says, "Oils are my favorite". She loves working outdoors and often uses her digital camera to capture the moment at a site. Carol is a member of the Central Kentucky Art Guild in Elizabethtown and was nominated Artist of the Year in 2000 and 2005. Over the years she has been painting, she has had 3 "one person" shows. Many of her paintings hang in private collections throughout the United States, England, Spain, Italy and Australia.

She is a juried member of Oil Painters of America, Kentucky Arts Council's Visual Arts at the Market, and Central Kentucky Art Guild. Her work consistently is included in juried and invitational shows across the region.

Amidst all this creative activity Carol has just obtained her private pilots license. She is also an amateur radio operator and holds a 1st class Radio Telecommunications license.

She and her partner of 31 years own and operate a computer business which she says is easier to run now that she has a home studio. They also own Trinity Music Productions promoting acoustic guitar masters and produce the concert series that are held at Hardin County Schools Performing Arts Center. http://www.acousticguitarmasters.com

Carol takes an active roll in promoting art in her community. She provides personal leadership that encourages and supports individual artists and bolsters collaboration among regional arts agencies.

You can see many of Carol's fine paintings at www.carolreesor.com or call for an appointment for a private viewing at 270 325 3958.

It

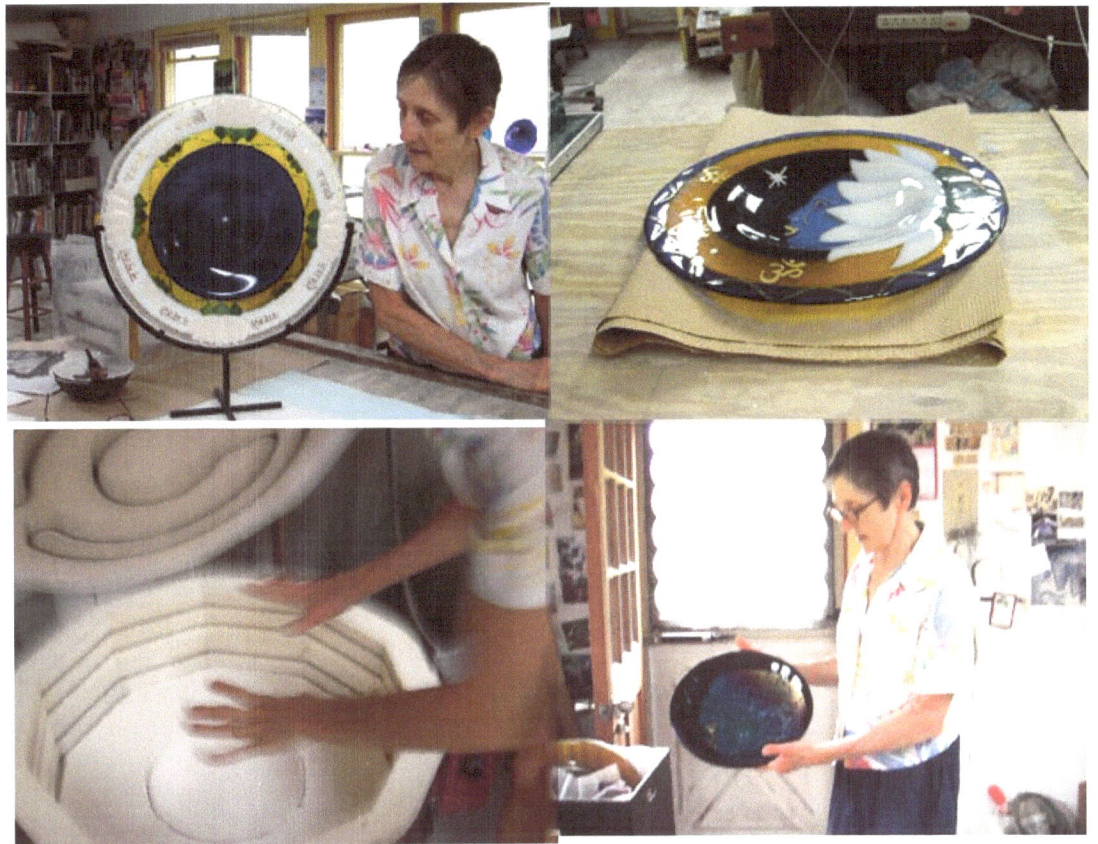

was over the dry creek bed and through the woods, and through the woods and through the woods before entering the magical world where Kathy Zajac lives with her stained glass artist husband, Joe Larson.

Kathy Zajac, a native of Cleveland, Ohio has lived in Hart County for 30 years after she and Joe moved here from California. Really nestled in a wooded paradise they reside in peace and harmony with the land in a beautiful, functional home they have built with their own hands. They have also built their out buildings and Home Studio Art Glass, their studio where they work their magic. Joe is a stained glass artisan, also working in fused and slumped glass and Kathy, who now basically works solely in fused and slumped glass.

Kathy says in 1981 she worked in stained glass, mostly cutting and grinding for Joe. In 1990 she started learning the process of fused glass, taking many courses including a prestigious course in Corning New York. Now she produces incredible "one of a kind" works of art that have a Zen-like quality to them; functional and decorative art glass pieces that one can use in one's home.

Fused glass is similar to working in stained glass as one will cut the glass in the pattern one wants. However, the fusing is done in 2 layers. Kathy says, "The process is very special and the glass has to be compatible when you fuse two pieces together. There are many different production methods and recipes for making glass. As a result, there are almost as many different types of glass as there are glass artists who want to use them. Types of glass range from basic window glass (called "float glass") to brightly colored stained glass (also called "art glass"), and many of the types of glass come in numerous sub-types and categories. In addition, there are many types of glass coatings, such as iridescent and dichroic, which have unique properties when applied to glass. New types of glass and glass coatings are constantly being developed.

All of these different glass types are candidates for fusing, slumping, and other warm glass processes. Some can be used off the shelf, but others require testing to make sure they will work in the kiln. That's because it's likely that an artist will want to combine more than one different sheet of glass in their projects. If so, then the artist needs to make sure the glass they select is "compatible." Using incompatible glass may cause cracking or even shattering of the piece when it cools."

To better understand compatibility, let's consider what happens when glass gets heated in a kiln. Like many other substances, glass expands when it gets hot and contracts when it cools. This change in density, which occurs at the molecular level, can be measured in a laboratory. A typical one inch piece of Bullseye brand glass, for example, will expand 0.0000090 inches for each 1 degree Centigrade (about 1.8 degrees Fahrenheit) increase in temperature. That's nine-millionths of an inch! This rate, which is commonly known as the Coefficient of Expansion (COE), is usually expressed as a whole number, rather than as a long decimal figure. Most Bullseye glass, for example, is said to have a Coefficient of Expansion of 90, and you will often hear glass artists refer to it as COE90 glass. Spectrum, another common glass, has a COE of around 96, while Corning's Pyrex glassware has a 32 COE. Standard window glass, referred to as "float" glass by the glassmaking community, has a COE that is usually around 84-87, while Effetre (Moretti) glass, commonly used for lampworking, has a 104 COE.

Kathy also works with the slumping glass method. Slumping is an expanded method of working in fused glass. Molds for slumping can be used in several different ways, but the most common are slumping into and slumping over the mold. Slumping into the mold is probably the most widely used way to slump as this approach allows the glass to sag into the mold. Shapes frequently formed in this manner include bowls and platters. The molds used in this way need to have small holes in the bottom in order to allow the air to escape when the glass slumps.

With slumping over the mold one uses this approach, in which the glass is allowed to fall over the outside of the mold, generally uses molds made of stainless steel. Because bowls and vases made using this technique tend to be characterized by their wavy sides (like folds of cloth), slumping over the mold is sometimes called "draping."

One very important thing to keep in mind is that molds that are used for slumping into (rather than over) need to have holes drilled in the bottom. This is to allow air to escape from the mold as the glass slumps into place. Without the holes, air will be trapped underneath the glass and it will not be able to slump properly.

Commercial molds for commonly slumped forms such as bowls and plates are widely available and the Larson's have many of them. Molds can be made of materials as diverse as stainless steel, pottery clay, or plaster/silica mixtures. I discovered that one can even use found objects, like auto hubcaps or terra cotta pots, as molds. Some molds need to be covered with kiln wash before they can be used; others are ready "as is." I also discovered that some materials do NOT make good molds. Copper and aluminum won't work; they will either melt or deform badly in the heat of the kiln. Steel sometimes works, but it is likely to oxidize or even warp. Cast iron may work, but it is very heavy and prone to rust. Stainless steel is by far the easiest and most available material to use for metal molds. Most commercially available molds are made of either vitreous clay or stainless steel. Other kinds of molds generally need to be mixed and shaped by the artist.

Kathy told me that the basic fusing and slumping process has five main stages:
 1. Heating phase - where the temperature increases from room temperature to the temperature where fusing and slumping takes place. The "heating" phase, which takes place between room temperature and around 1200 to 1700 degrees F (depending on the process you are performing), is where the glass makes the transition from a solid to a more flowing form. As glass is heated and moves through this phase, it goes through three separate states. First, from room temperature up to about 1000 degrees F (540 degrees C), glass remains rigid and brittle. It is expanding slowly, but will still crack or break if the temperature increases too rapidly. This kind of temperature related fracture is called "thermal shock." How rapid is rapid enough to cause thermal shock? The answer depends on several factors, but the most important are the thickness of the glass and the width of the piece of glass. By the time the temperature of the glass gets above 1000 degrees F, any glue, moisture, or surface contaminants have burned off. The glass begins to soften slightly and the surface of the glass will look glossy. Thermal shock will not occur at this temperature.

When the temperature reaches around 1300 to 1400 degrees F, the glass gradually becomes soft enough to conform to a mold. It starts to glow a bright yellowish-red. The edges may soften and round and two pieces of glass that are touching will begin to stick together. This is the temperature range where slumping takes place. If heating continues above 1330 degrees F and moves toward 1500 degrees F (820 C), the color of the glass deepens and becomes redder. Glass in this range has slumped completely and even starts to stretch out of shape.

Full fusing, the complete merging of two or more pieces of glass into one, takes place at around 1500 degrees F. Above that temperature, glass becomes increasingly liquid. Kiln casting and pate de verre take place in this range. As the temperature moves above 1500 degrees F, glass also glows bright red. Bubbles may move toward the surface of the glass and pop. By the time the temperature reaches around 1700 degrees F (925 C), the glass is buttery and can be moved when prodded with a tool. The technique of manipulating molten glass with a tool is called "combing" or "raking". Glass manipulation techniques should be undertaken with care and only after you have some experience with fusing and slumping.

2. Soaking phase - where the temperature is maintained at a given point for a period of time The "Soaking" phase generally occurs at the highest temperature in the cycle. This temperature is around 1500 degrees Fahrenheit for fusing or around 1200 - 1300 degrees for slumping, but it can be higher or lower for different processes such as fire polishing, combing, or casting. The length of the soak time can also vary.

When one is slumping, longer soak times cause the glass to conform more closely to the mold. When one is fusing, longer soak times cause the piece to become flatter and smoother. How long to soak also depends on other factors, such as type of glass, the thickness of the glass, the final shape desired, and how long the kiln has taken to make it through the heating phase. Soaking can last as short as a minute or as long as an hour or more.

3. Rapid cooling phase - when the temperature is quickly dropped from its highest point to just above the annealing range and it comes after soaking, when the glass has taken on the desired shape, the process enters the "Rapid Cooling" phase. This involves cooling the glass as quickly as possible until the red color goes away and the natural color starts to come back. Generally, rapid cooling is accomplished by lifting the lid of the kiln for a few seconds and allowing some of the hot air to escape. This can be a risky maneuver, so it's a good idea to wear gloves and be especially careful while the kiln is open.
The major reason for the rapid cooling phase (as well as for the rapid temperature increase at the end of the heating phase) is to reduce the amount of time the glass spends above 1300 degrees Fahrenheit. Glass left too long in this zone has a tendency to devitrify, or take on a scummy, generally unattractive surface appearance that is difficult, if not impossible, to reverse.

Devitrification is when glass molecules start to crystallize. It usually takes the appearance of a whitish scum on the top edge of the glass being fired. Most glass artists consider it to be a nuisance to be avoided, but some like the effect and use it in their glass projects. It is most likely to occur above 1300F (usually around 1350 to 1400 degrees F); for this reason, it's a good idea to minimize the time glass spends around that temperature. Some glasses are more prone to devitrification than others and some, such as the "tested compatible" glass manufactured by Bullseye, Uroboros, and Spectrum, have been especially formulated to resist devitrification.

4. Annealing phase is the critical step that relieves the stress in the glass. Once the Rapid Cooling phase is complete and color has started to return to the glass, the kiln has cooled to approximately 1050 degrees Fahrenheit and the "annealing" phase begins. Annealing is a process by which the stress in the glass is relieved and the molecules in the glass are allowed to cool and arrange themselves into a solid, stable form. Successful annealing is the key to creating glasswork that will remain stable once it cools to room temperature.
Unlike many substances, glass does not melt or harden at a single temperature. Instead, it gradually softens and hardens as the temperature changes. The phase during which this transition from liquid to solid occurs is called the "annealing zone."

5. Cool to room temperature phase - where the glass gradually becomes cool enough to touch. Once annealing is complete, the Cooling to Room Temperature phase begins. Often this is no more complicated than simply allowing the kiln to cool naturally, but thicker pieces of glass and kilns that cool rapidly require a bit more attention. The key is to slow down the rate of cooling so that thermal shock is prevented and the glass cools without cracking. Probably the most important factor in how quickly you can cool the glass is the overall size and thickness of the glass being cooled. Very small pieces can generally be cooled as rapidly as desired, but larger pieces need more time to cool. For example, a 12" (30 cm) diameter 1/8" (3 mm) thick glass can safely cool from 750 degrees F to room temperature in 40 minutes. Doubling the thickness to 1/4" (6 mm) doubles the time required to 80 minutes and 3/8" thick glass requires at least two hours to cool to room temperature.

I learned if ones kiln retains heat very well; the natural cooling rate of the kiln may be sufficiently slow. In some cases, however, one may need to intermittently fire the kiln to slow down the rate of cooling.

Kathy uses a large glass firing kiln which is unlike a ceramic kiln as it has coils in the lid also, thus enabling the production of even heat all around the piece she is working on.

This lady really knows her stuff and together with Joe they create some of the most beautiful art glass bowls and plates I have ever seen. It is this writer's opinion that Kathy's work is world class art glass, as is Joes, but this article is about Kathy.

The pieces are modestly priced starting at $200.00 and one can buy them right at their studio at 1335 Sam Goodman Rd., Munfordville, KY by appointment only. Call Kathy at 270 524 0757. Getting there is not for the faint of heart, but once you have your appointment, get ready to be awed, amazed and impressed with these beautiful pieces of art glass that are being produced right here in little ole Munfordville, KY!

Meet Kentucky artist Mary Sego

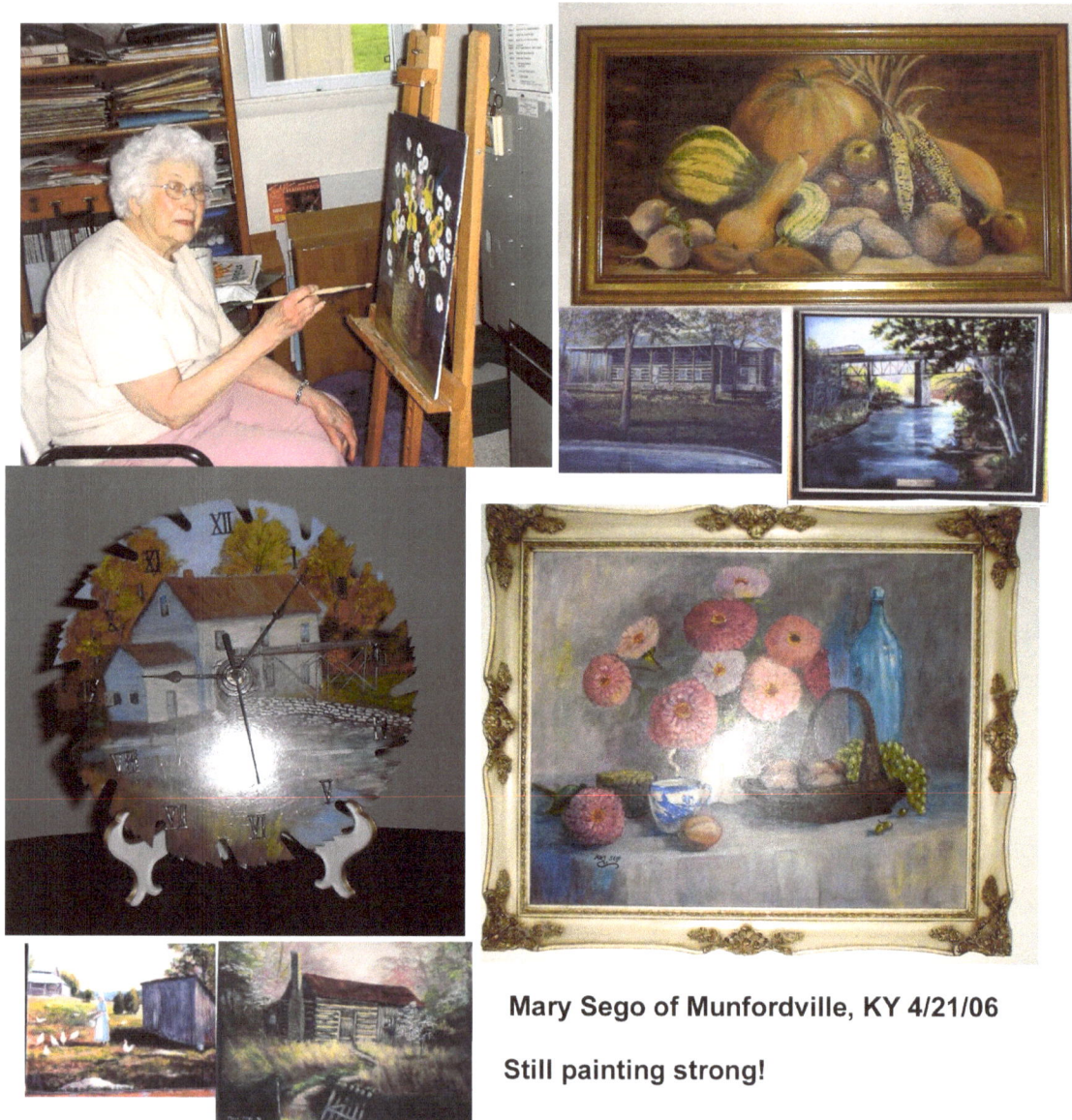

Mary Sego of Munfordville, KY 4/21/06

Still painting strong!

Each week I am constantly amazed by the amount of artistic talent that I come across and this week I had the delightful pleasure to meet Mary Sego of 510 Elk St. in Munfordville, KY. It seems that Hart County is full of talented people!

As far as I am concerned Mary Sego should be called one of Hart County's National Treasures!

Mary is in her 80's, has just recovered fully from a heart attack, is still an active school bus monitor who is looking forward to retiring at the end of this school year so she can devote more time to painting and all the other things she feels she wants to do.

A native of Munfordville, she married when she was 16, raised her family and didn't start painting until 1976 when she was into her second marriage. Her husband wanted to give Mary something special for that Christmas and since she had been drawing since she could hold a crayon as a young child, she told him she wanted art supplies. He told her to buy what she wanted and he would pay for it. She went into Glasgow to a store and bought a "How to Paint with Acrylics" by Walter Foster. She read it from cover to cover and started working in acrylics with her new paints, brushes, canvases and easel.

Mary has since gone on to further educate herself as a "self taught" artist and graduated from acrylics to watercolors to pastels. Many of her paintings sell quickly and she has won many awards over the years.

I asked Mary what her favorite medium was and she said, "Acrylics as they get less "muddy" than oils. I like water colors also, but they are not as "forgiving" as the other mediums. Once I make a mistake in water colors, I usually have to discard the painting as most times it can not be repaired as I can in the other mediums. I do mostly landscapes and still lives"

Mary went on to say, "I paint on anything, shovels, mailboxes, saw blades, glass, trinket boxes, you name it. Years ago I used to be a weaver."

She paints many of her wonderful paintings from memories of her life on a KY farm. She sometimes works with a digital camera when she has it with her. She uses her utility room as a studio which she laughingly says she shares with her washer and dryer.

Mary says, "Riding on the school bus as a monitor for 2.5 hours twice a day, I get to see a lot of local landscape in all four seasons. My memory is still good and I sketch it when I get home in the afternoon. I love those lovely old fences and gates, the old bumpy country roads. I guess it is in my blood to paint and I have many things I still want to do."

Well, I guess Mary has been doing it and hopefully will continue to do it. Her paintings are historical records of Hart County and their timeless beauty will give pleasure to those who have the opportunity to see them.

Mary's paintings can be seen by appointment only. Just give her a call at 270 524 4411. Her smaller paintings start at $150.00.

Meet Kentucky artists Bill and Vennie Beeler

Bill Beeler is a native of KY who was raised in Bardstown. Vennie Beeler is native of Tahoka, TX and together this husband and wife art team lives in Elizabethtown, KY. Bill is a retired Civil Service Education Specialist who worked at Fort Knox. Vennie retired as a

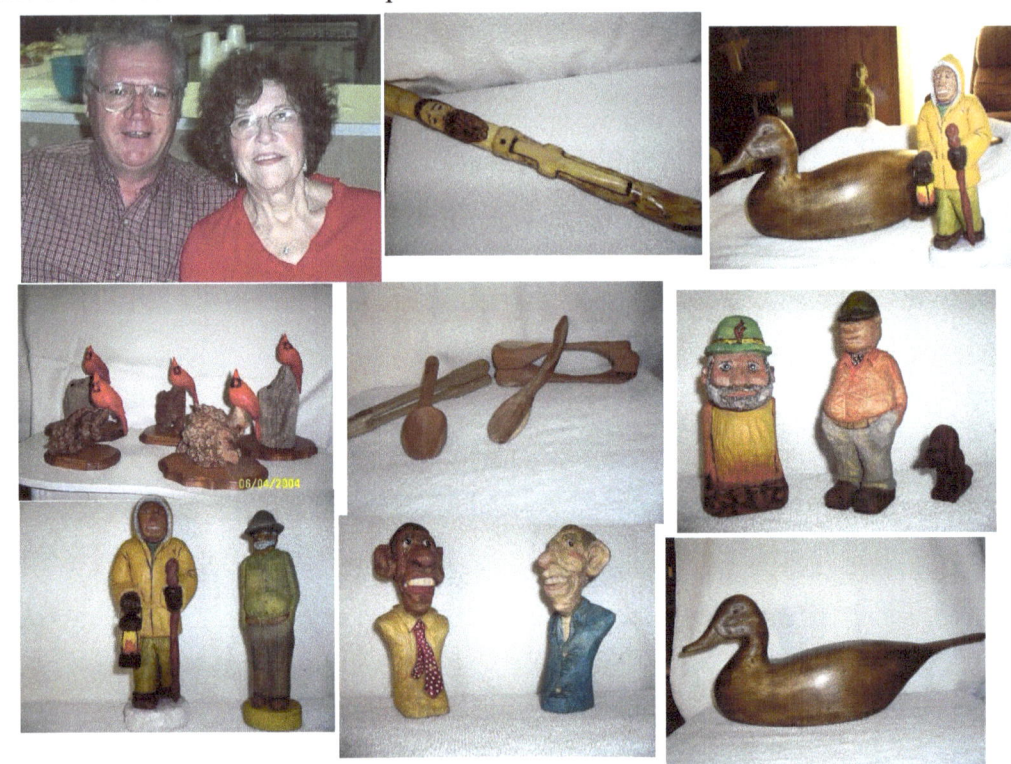

director of Family Child Care.

Bill got into wood carving about 3 years ago while spending the winters in Punta Gorda, FL. Vennie has been painting ever since she was a little girl who received a gift of a watercolor set and coloring book. She says her mother kept her supplied with paint brushes made from the hair of cow's tails.

Vennie paints mostly in oils and watercolors. She has been juried by the Central KY Art Guild and she also started to carve birds 2 years ago.

Bill does a lot of carving and does walking sticks and spoons and characters. Since his cornea operation Vennie has taking to do the final painting on Bill's carvings.

Both are members of the National Wood Carvers Association and the Charlotte County Wood Carvers Association in Charlotte FL.

Bill says, "I like working with cedar for my spoons and characters and I have to be very careful because cedar is toxic. I search out twisted Sassafras for my walking sticks and both are always watching out for scrap wood, especially KY woods."

His finished pieces are rubbed with tongue oil except for the spoons that are finished in mineral oil. The painted pieces, Vennie finishes in acrylic paints.

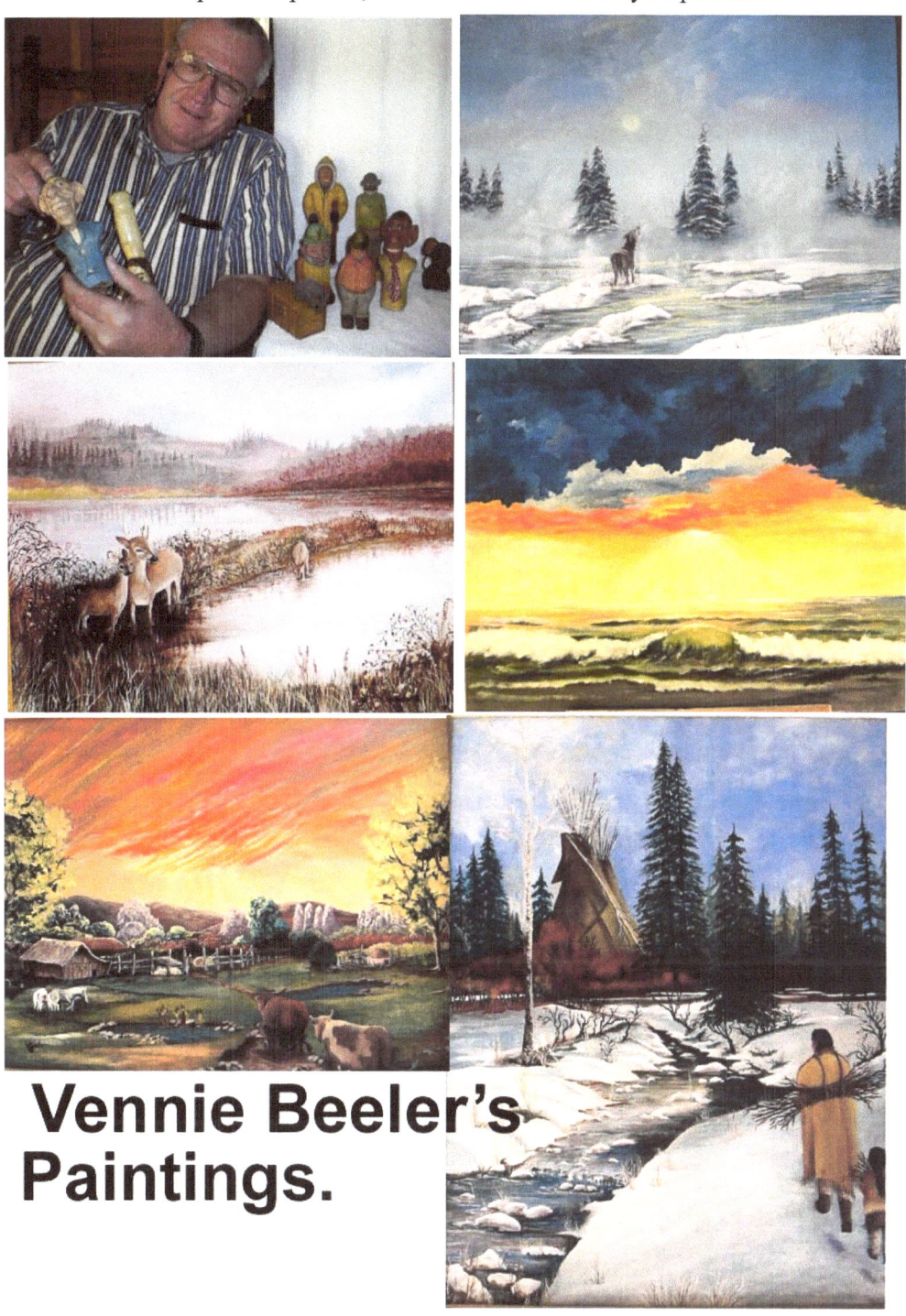

Vennie Beeler's Paintings.

They both say, "They don't finish any pieces with olive oil or vegetable oil as it will go rancid." Vennie's paintings are brilliant in color and have masterful feelings.
One can call them at 270 769 5685 to view their paintings and carvings by appointment only.

Meet Kentucky artist Leslie Blackford.

Leslie Blackford works in Polymer Clay and has for 13 years. She lives in Priceville

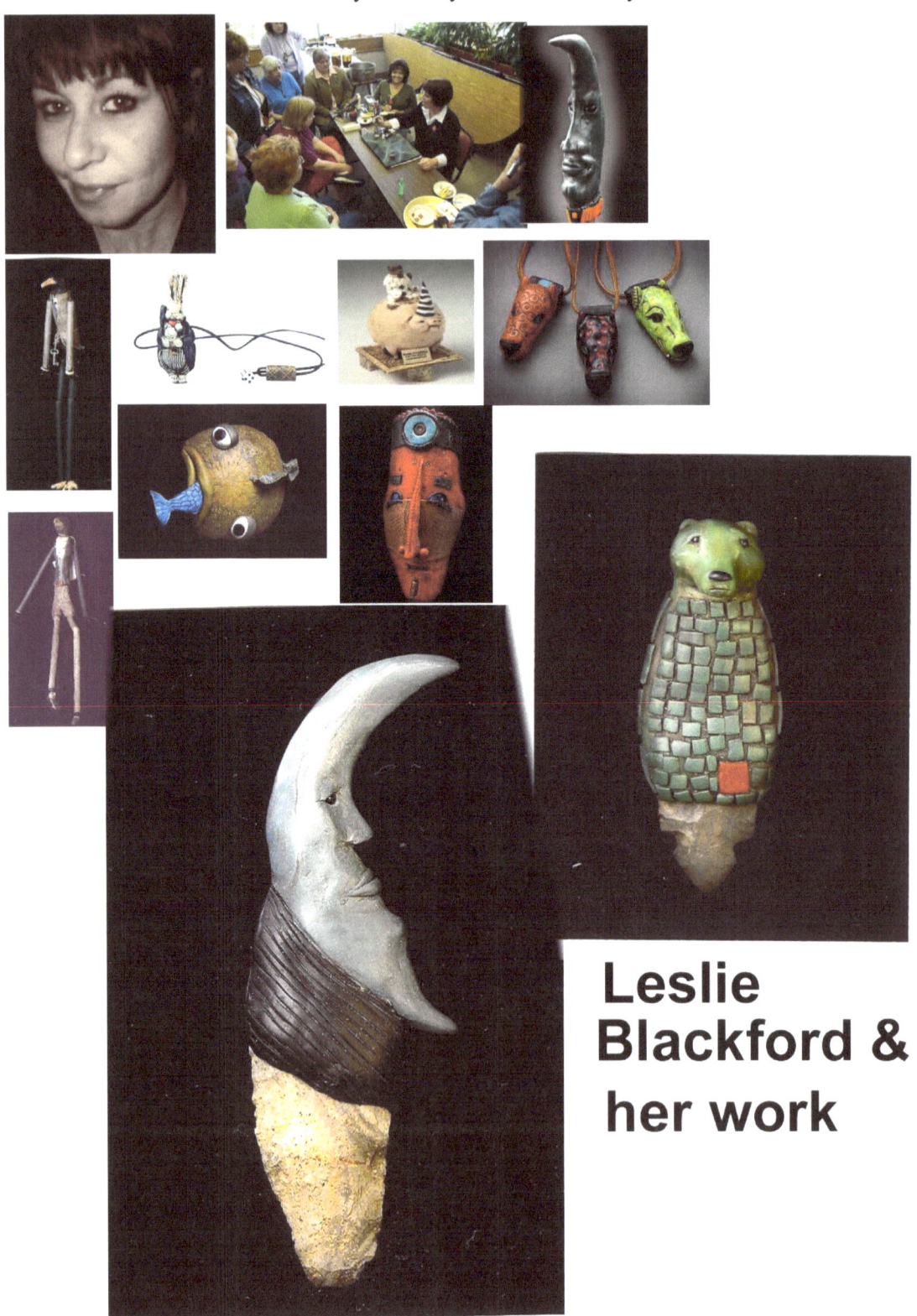

**Leslie
Blackford &
her work**

and has lived in Hart County since she was 14 years of age.

When I asked her how she got involved with working in Polymer Clay she said, "A friend introduced me and from the moment I touched the clay I was hooked. After I perfected my craft I wanted to share it with others and the company owner that makes the clay approached me to go to shows and teach workshops."

Leslie is very involved in working with and teaching others to work with Polymer clay. She has been teaching for 3 years and she currently teaches this craft in 7 schools in Hart Co. Kentucky.

She makes masks, animal faces, lights from polymer when she does her free lance work at her studio at 1008 Doc Speevack Rd. Munfordville, KY 42567. She has done workshops and demonstrations in such places at Las Vegas, Chicago, Florida and recently returned from teaching a workshop in Nottingham, England.

She teaches many classes including a class in Hinged Animal Art. Leslie says, "Animals and nature have always been the place that I draw the most inspiration from. Each individual animal on earth has its own distinct feature that makes them what they are. In this class I would like to show the class how to sculpt any animal's face by focusing on just a few basic techniques. After everyone has created their own unique "animal head" we will continue to make a body, arms and legs for the art doll. I will encourage the class to let the creative mind take over the project. I intend for this class to open their imaginations back to when they were a children. To a time when they had no preconceived notions of the way things are supposed to be and give in to whimsy and playfulness. I will show the class how to attach each limb with buna cord to complete the animal. Each student should leave the class with a totally unique work of art made from polymer clay."

When one works with Polymer Clay it has to be conditioned and one can condition it by simply working the clay with your hands until it reaches a good working consistency. The warmth of your hands combined with the physical process of stretching and compressing the clay changes its texture, making it softer and more pliable.

There are several brands of Polymer Clay to choose from. However, for making beads or covering objects, any of the polymer clay brands does fine. However, if you're making objects (such as boxes, picture frames, etc) from clay, or creating buttons or thin pieces that must hold up to handling, you'll want to select a strong clay such as Fimo, Promat, or Cernit. If you want to use weaker clay such as Sculpey for such pieces, first make the base piece from strong clay, and then apply the weaker clay as a veneer over it.
You really do not need any special equipment to fire your finished product whether it is a small statue, beads or whatever you are making. You regular kitchen oven will do the trick.

Recommendations on this vary, and you'll notice that different brands of clay call for different firing temperatures. It's a good idea to get an oven thermometer and use it to determine the actual temperature your oven gives. The oven temperature must reach at least 210° Fahrenheit or so for the polymer to fuse properly; if the temperature goes above 300° Fahrenheit, the clay may burn, giving off dangerous fumes.

Within these limits, any temperature will work, although you should avoid firing Sculpey translucent, Fimo art translucent, and possibly other translucent clays at high temperatures, because it may change their color. Manufacturers recommend temperatures between 250 and 275° Fahrenheit for all except transparent clays.

The firing time depends mainly on the thickness of your pieces. For clay a quarter of an inch thick, 20 minutes is plenty; for thicker pieces you may need to go up to an hour to get maximum strength. Apparently you do not even need to preheat the oven.

You can use polymer clay without any special finishing treatment at all. The finish of polymer clay right after firing varies by brand - Fimo has a slight gloss, Sculpey has a matte finish, Cernit is slightly waxy-looking. For many pieces, you may find that the clay's natural finish best enhances the effect you want. For other pieces, you may prefer the shinier or glossier finish available with various finishing techniques such as wet-sanding, buffing, and glazing. Buffing produces a deeper, more subtle sheen; glazing produces a harder shine and takes considerably less time.

Polymer Clay can be purchased via the internet or just call Leslie at 531 5853 to go to the local workshops she teaches here in Munfordville or join the Polymer Clay Guild that meets once a month in Munfordville. They have 14 members and they all enjoy this craft.

Meet Kentucky artist Jim Cantrell

Once in a blue moon one gets to meet a really great living artist and this past week I met Jim Cantrell of Bardstown. Jim says, "I am not an artist, I am a painter and before that I was a potter and before that I was an educator."

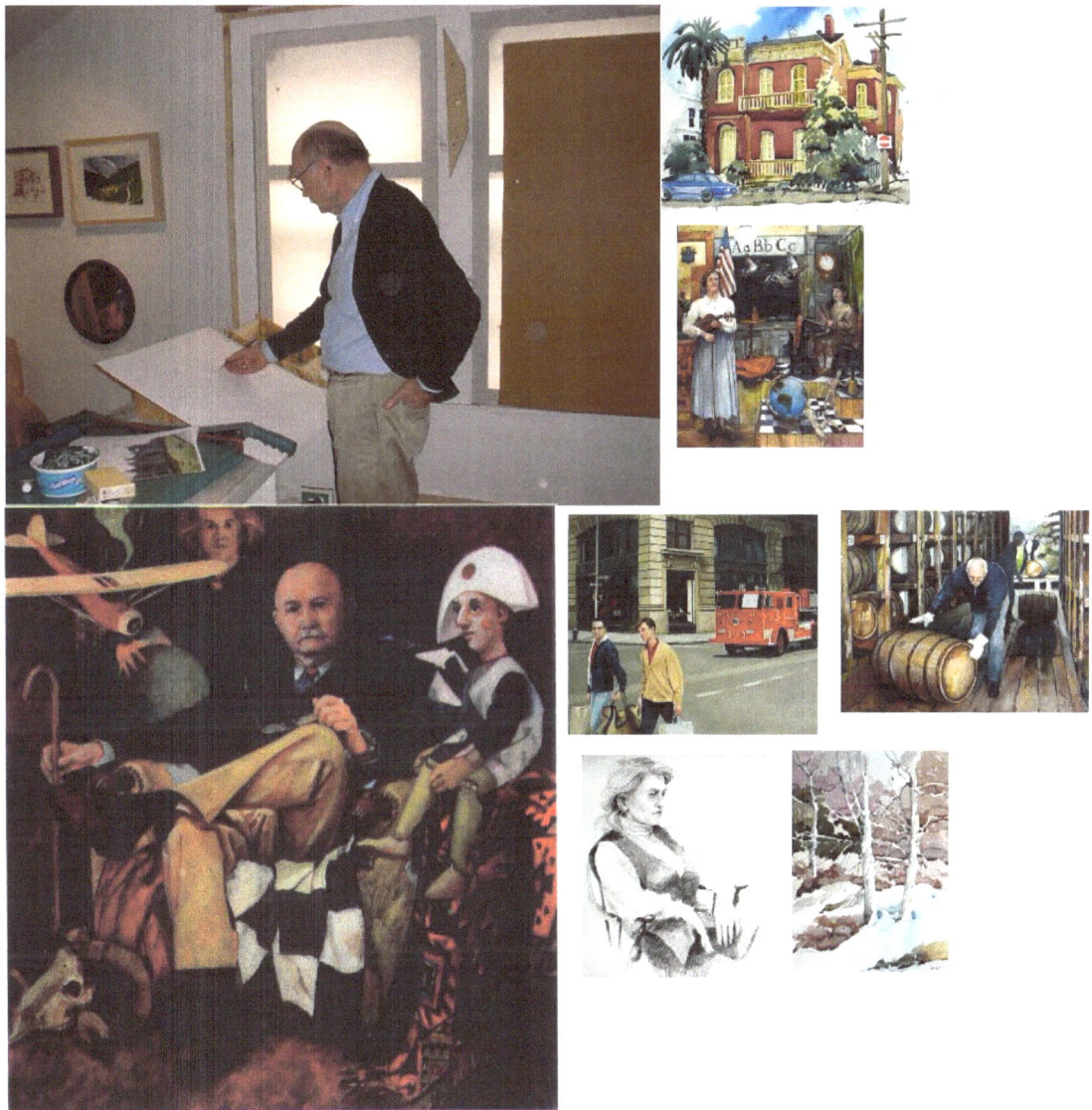

A native of Oklahoma and raised in eastern Nebraska, Cantrell earned his Bachelor of Fine Arts degree from the University of Nebraska at Lincoln in 1958 and his Master of Arts degree from the University of Northern Colorado in Greeley in 1965 with a double emphasis in ceramics & painting. He began his distinguished career as a teacher. In 1971 he established himself as an independent studio artist in Bardstown, Kentucky where he continues to work.

Jim Cantrell paints primarily with oils and watercolors. He describes his technique as abstracted realism. His forte is the human figure encompassing masterful composition, & technique.

Upon visiting this artist, I found him outside his home building awnings on his back patio. Jim says he enjoys building things more than anything else. The house Jim works in serves as an incredible art gallery, studio and living quarters for both Jim and his lovely wife Jeannette and is full of Jim's paintings as well as other artist's works. Many beautiful pieces of pottery are still on display from when Jim had a successful pottery studio. Jim says," I changed over to painting when the clay got too heavy to lift and also during that time pottery sales went down and painting sales went up!" Well, pottery's loss is the art world's gain.

Jim says, "I am pretty much of a loner and really do not have much to do with people, yet I really enjoy painting people." That statement is truly apparent in his works and a trip out to his studio is well worth the time.

Jim is a self taught watercolorist and his work is very brilliant. At one time he was the Resident Artist at Berea, but after one year he decided that it was not his cup of tea.

Prior to settling in Bardstown, Jim says, "I dragged my wife and 2 children all over the place looking for a community that we would feel comfortable in and in 1971 we drove into Bardstown and felt this was the place. We rented an old building to open the Bardstown Pottery & Gallery in November 1971 and there we worked and lived until we purchased the Roby house in 1997 which is our present location." Between 1971 and 1997 there was a lot of work and discomfort for Jim and his family in the beginning. No water in the original building, many renovations, having to basically sleep next to the kilns to make sure the firings was correct. He says, "Our 2 children swore they would never get into art, but they are!"

Jim's exhibitions and paintings are too numerous to list here, but you can take my word that this painter is not to be overlooked. Make sure you put it on your list to go over to see his works. You will be glad you did.

Jim's wife, Jeannette says, "The Bardstown Art Gallery opened in 1971 in Spalding Hall, the site of a defunct boarding school for boys in Bardstown, Kentucky. After 26 years in that location the gallery moved to its present location, a 1930's Arts & Crafts bungalow, on West Stephen Foster Ave. We are now the oldest private gallery in Kentucky.

The gallery handles contemporary works in the mediums of oil paintings, works on paper, collage & assemblage, ceramics, photographs, and glicees by regional artists of merit. Quarterly exhibitions are scheduled with prices ranging from one hundred dollars to several thousands of dollars. Gallery Hours are By Chance or By Appointment. We live in the building and are usually here Tuesday through Saturday from 10:30 am-5:00 pm and it is a good idea to call ahead to make certain we are here or to arrange a visit during our "off hours". Business necessitates our being absent at times, but we really do want to accommodate your needs. So don't hesitate to call!"

Bardstown Art Gallery   www.bardstownartgallery.com
214 West Stephen Foster Ave.
Bardstown, KY 40004
Phone: 502.348.6488
cantrell@bardstownartgallery.com

Meet Kentucky artist Donna Seymour

Writing this column is not only fun it is truly educational. Every week I have the opportunity to learn something new and this week is no different when I went to interview local artist Donna Seymour.

A native of Barren County, Donna and her husband Randy returned here after working and living in Tennessee. They live in Upton and own and operate Roundstone Native Seed which is your local source for native warm season grass seed and prairie restoration services.

Donna is an artist of many, many talents and all of them done really very well. She is a watercolor artist, quilt maker, doll maker and a creator of the age old tradition of floor cloths.

When I asked Donna how she got started making floor cloths she said about 4 years ago she and a few friends got together to make some. When they were finished her friends ended making them and she has continued.

Donna says, "The use of painted canvas floor coverings, also known as *"oyl cloths"* dates as far back as the 14th century in Europe. When people came to this country they were looking for ways to reproduce some of the furnishings they were used to back home. Resources were limited, but worn sails from ships provided them with a base to paint and cover the floor with American primitive paintings which often depict subjects standing on boldly geometric floor cloths." This writer had heard of floor cloths and later learned that William Burnet, Governor of New York and Massachusetts during Colonial times, had floor cloths listed in his household inventory; and later, George Washington ordered floor cloths for his Mt. Vernon retirement home. Canvas was more readily available than other rug and carpet supplies, and the ease of cleaning made floor cloths particularly desirable. Placed over wide boards, the heavily painted canvases cut cold drafts from below, and were cool underfoot in summer.

Donna says, "Over time floor cloths proved themselves to be one of the most durable forms of floor covering used. Centuries-old pieces still remain intact, with the pattern clearly visible." Today, Donna's floor cloths are made from the same 100% cotton heavyweight canvas (with a sewn hem and mitered corners). Environmentally-safe, water-based paints and finishes are used in place of yellowing varnishes and slow-drying paints of years ago. Each of her floor cloths is put through a series of steps to ensure a finished piece which will lie flat and maintain its shape, colors and finish for years to come. First she paints the canvas with Gesso to give it body, and then she paints her pictures on it. Finally, with 3 to 6 coats of extremely durable (yet still flexible) polyurethane protecting each painted piece, Donna's floor cloths will stand up to the most demanding traffic- from children to dogs, heavy furniture to sloppy eaters. Her last step is to wax them with Johnson paste wax. She says, "Just damp mop with a mild cleanser and apply a floor wax to restore the finish from time to time." I learned

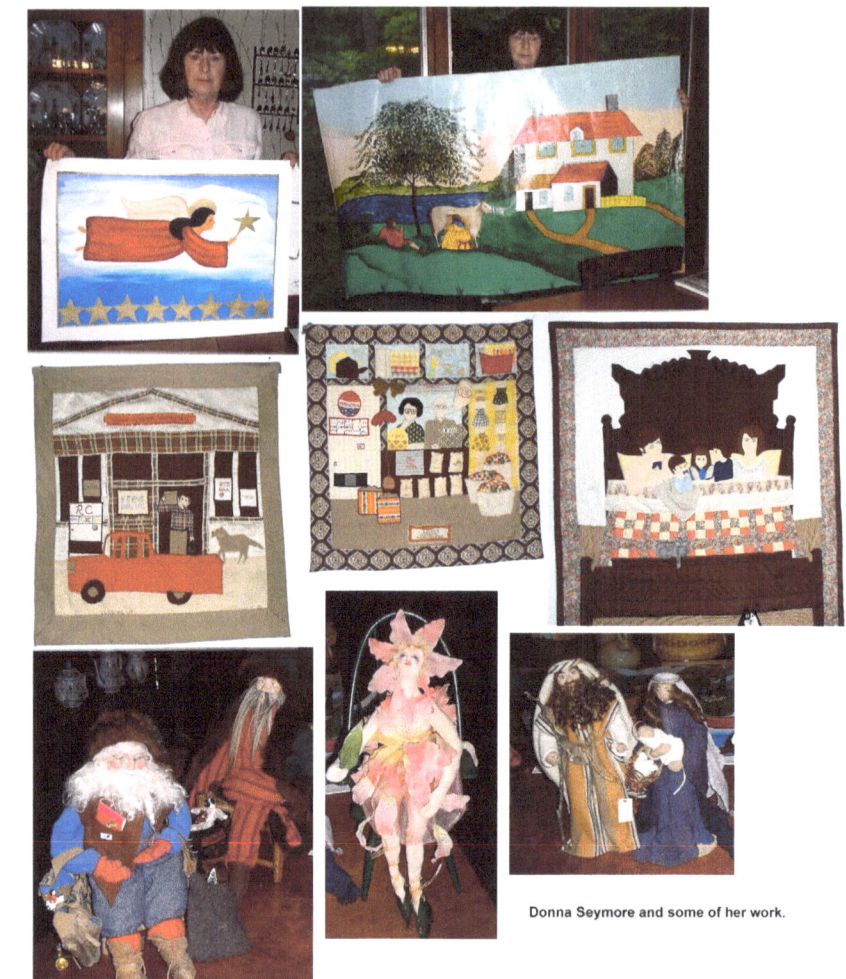

Donna Seymore and some of her work.

that smaller pieces can be adhered to the floor with poster adhesive or double-sided carpet tape. Larger pieces can be unrolled and used without any particular installation." Donna teaches a workshop on making floor cloths.

Donna then showed me the magnificent dolls she makes. The faces and limbs are made of polymer clay, usually a brand called Scumpy. The faces start out as a ball of foil and then the polymer clay is laid over it and molded into a face that is usually personalized. The bodies are a wire frame and she makes all the clothes including the fur coats from clothing that her friends have given her over the years. She uses all natural fibers, leathers and furs. The hair and beards are mohair fibers. Her dolls can be special ordered and run in price from $150.00 to $350.00.each. She has been making them for about 15 years and they sell quite quickly.

Donna says, "As to my watercolor paintings, I am a self taught painter who usually works in my kitchen. I have taken some watercolor workshops through the Glasgow Chamber of Commerce and I once took a basket making workshop at Arrowmount in Gatlinburg, TN."

Donna has the ability to weave memories into her work. This is quite evident in the handmade wall hangings she has made of her mother's general store and one she made of when her 3 children were little and all used to pile into their parents big bed.

You can order a floor cloth or a handmade doll from Donna Seymour by calling 270 531 2353.

Meet Kentucky artist Mark Allen Brent

Artist, crafter, woodworker, Mark Allen Brent weaves them all using pieces of his and his ancestors past to create the most interesting works of folk art.

Folk art is usually made by people who have had little or no formal schooling in art. Folk artists generally make works of art with traditional techniques and content, in styles handed down through many generations, and often of a particular region. Paintings, sculptures, ceramics, metalwork, costume, tools, and other everyday objects all may be folk art then with this in mind; Mark Allen Brent is a true Folk Artist.

Mark, a native of Munfordville, lives in Cub Run with his wife Judy Lynn and his two daughters Kasey age 10 and Macenzie age 8.

Mark says he always drew as a child, especially cartoons. Though he took some art courses such as silk screening and advertising art design when a student in Munfordville High School, he basically is a self taught artist.

He enjoys bringing history alive in his work. When he makes his birdhouses, he makes two kinds. One kind is the authentic birdhouse which the birds enjoy and inhabit throughout the wooded area of his home. The other is the memorable decorative ones he makes that may signify the general store, homestead, church or building from one of his ancestors lives. These are quite intricate and elaborate and are usually made from a piece of wood or metal that came from the original subject matter. Thereby lays the historical thread he weaves into that piece of folk art.

He likes to utilize old antiques from his family's past such as an old flat iron that belonged to his mother which he hand decorated when he painted a picture of her on it.

Mark hand paints gourds, makes Christmas ornaments and does just about anything you can think of. It seems no piece of wood, metal or glass can be passed by. He recycles history! He paints large wall murals and carves the smallest owls I have ever seen out of black walnut shells. He says the smaller the piece he is working on the better he likes it.

He showed me a hand painted wooden fireplace screen he made from wood from his wife's homestead and it was in front of the mantel he restored from his wife's family home that now graces one of the rooms in their home.

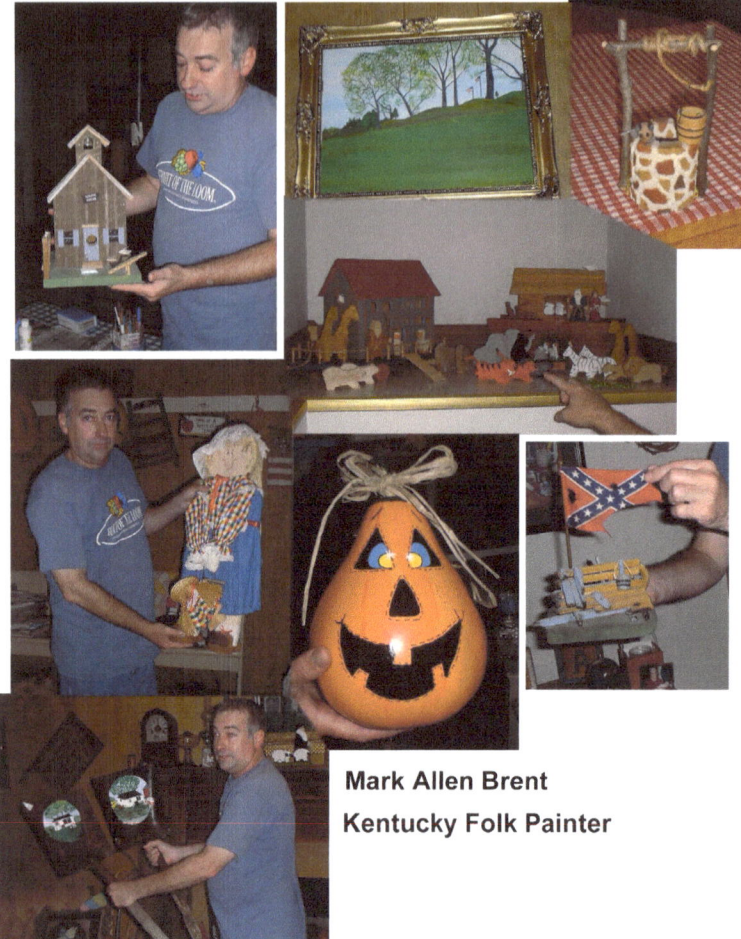

There are so many things he has made that it would fill a book to describe them and each one is a true folk art item with a story to it.

He currently is teaching his two young daughters the art of Folk Art Painting and the history that surrounds it and the pieces he uses.

So the next time you have something from your families past that you are getting ready to discard, look long and hard at it. Then bring your dad's old saw, shovel, ladder, your mom's antique ironing board or whatever to Mark Allen Brent as he can be hired to turn it into an heirloom folk art memento for you. You can reach him at his studio shop by calling 270 524 2598.

Mark Allen Brent
Kentucky Folk Painter

Meet Kentucky artist James Paul Walton

Over in the picturesque village of Hiseville, KY lives a shy and retiring artist named James Paul Walton. James, a bachelor, is a native of Hiseville and Barren County, born there on February 5, 1924.

He says he was a house painter by trade and left to go to Tucson, AZ for awhile and then to Springfield, IL only to return to his homestead.

James is a self-taught artist and started to paint in 1970 as a hobby. His first paints and canvases were left over house paint and cardboard and then he moved on to hard board. Eventually he started to use oil paints, canvases and canvas board and he does a grand job. His perspective is good, his colors are sound and his themes are many. He said he tried acrylics once, but did not like them, so he went back to the oils.

He showed me the first two portraits he did and I immediately recognized Henry Kissinger and JFK. His style is quite folksy in many of his landscapes. His paintings of the Hatfield and McCoy's homestead came with a story about the start of the feud. James says he thinks they continue it just for the publicity.

His subjects cover horses, landscapes, people and some flowers.

It was quite hard to get him to pose for a picture because he is so shy and he says he doesn't like to have his picture taken. Many of his pictures are not hung on the walls and when I asked why he said he has so many pictures his walls would look like the walls had been shot with a shotgun full of nails. However, his niece, Donna Seymour says he is afraid that a nearby tree may fall on his house and destroy his paintings.

When I asked James if he ever sold his paintings, he said he had sold a couple, but mostly gave them away. When asked if he would sell any today, he politely said no! He is saving them for his nieces and nephews and other relatives when he passes on.

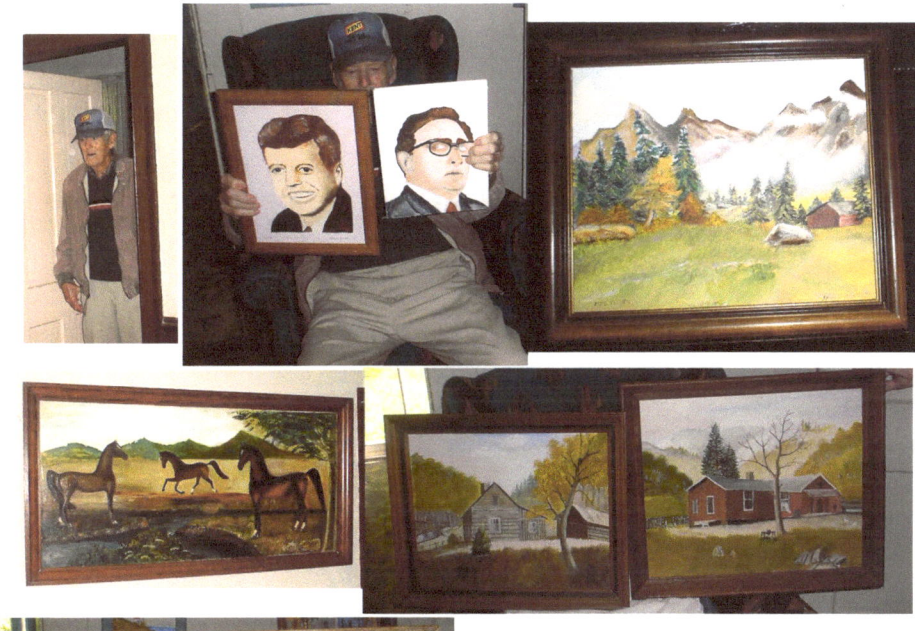

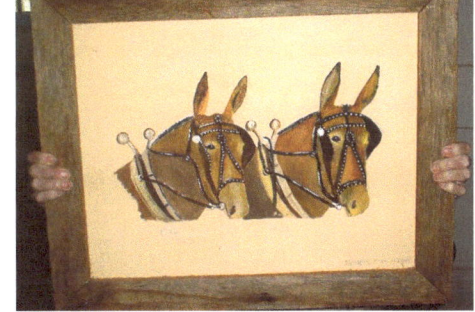

James Paul Walton of Hiseville KY

With some of his paintings.

5/23/06

James doesn't paint any longer since his cataract operation which left him with double vision. He says he misses being about to paint because it always made the time fly for him as he became totally absorbed in his work.

Though shy about displaying his works for an exhibit, he likes people to visit him and if you call him at 270 453 4372 he said he would be glad to show them to people.

Meet Kentucky artist Amy Seymour

Amy Seymour, a native of Michigan is a multi-talented gal who lives in Munfordville, KY. Not only is she the mother of an active and artistic 7 year old and a 10 year old, she teaches geography at UWK and is a Mammoth Cave tour guide, all of which makes her days pretty full.

However, like most of us she has a pretty incredible hobby to take the edge and stress off of everyday life and that hobby is working with Polymer Clay. This writer has seen a lot of polymer clay art lately, but none as lovely or as intricate as Amy's work.

Amy had just returned from the National Polymer Clay Guild retreat in Orkney Springs, VA which she has been regularly attending since 1998. She started working in Polymer clay in 1994 and has been a member of the KY-TN Polymer Clay Art Guild for the past 6 years.

Amy's intricate work basically starts with building up her clays to make a kaleidoscope of color into stout little blocks which she then stretches into longer blocks

Amy

Seymour & her

Polymer Clay Art

or tubs which she calls cane or caning. She then slices them into the sizes she wants which then are made into whatever she is designing.

I was totally amazed at the intricate designs she makes. One almost thinks they are made of blown or fused glass.

Amy says even though one can bake the clay in a kitchen oven, she feels with the amount of work she does, it would not be healthy for her family, so she has an old counter baking oven in her studio that is used primarily for the baking clay purpose only.

Amy went on to say that since Polymer Clay is a relatively new art form starting in the 70's she is pleased and proud to be able to work with and to personally know many of these art pioneers in this field.

She makes many things such as lovely jewelry, candle holders, Christmas ornaments, and trivets. One of her quilt designs for a trivet is shown in one of the Polymer Clay "bibles", Judy Belcher's book, "Polymer Clay Creative Traditions". She just made a special order of wall light switches to match the bedroom quilts in the buyer's home.

Amy belongs to a group who meets in Munfordville and surrounding areas once a month to share techniques, time and fellowship with each other and anyone interested in joining this group should call her.

When asked what would be the initial investment one would need to make to start working with Polymer Clay, Amy said one could start with a good palette of clay, a cutter and whatever else one needed for about $30.00. She indicated that an old ravioli grinder is a big help also and she showed me hers which had an electric motor attached to it. Amy is available for workshops and will create anything for you. You can visit her studio by appointment only by calling 270 524 5563. You may get her answering machine, but just leave a message and she will get back to you.

Meet Kentucky artist Eric Lindgren

One never knows when one is going to meet someone interesting. All I wanted was some information about a new professional printer for my studio and lo and behold I met a cartoonist!

Most people do not realize that drawing cartoons is often harder than painting a picture. Our society tends to associate cartoons with fun, humor, and often childhood, and this association is a positive one. By having fun, you can open up the creative pathways in your brain. I often thought of exploring the connection between Cartooning and Creativity. Just exactly what is a cartoon? I refer to drawings with or without captions used to illustrate, tell a joke, satirize, caricature, and entertain or to tell a story.

Cartooning is a fine example of the use of creative thinking. You can see a different perception of the world through the eyes of the cartoonist. Cartooning embraces many aspects of creativity and cartoons encapsulate all aspects of life - from the serious to the humorous, and from the mundane to big things of life. Humorous cartoons (this includes political cartoons) are combinations of drawings and words, or just drawings showing a situation. Cartoons used to illustrate books. It is amazing that books on creativity can be published without a single drawing or illustration! Cartoons appeal to the right-side of the brain, and their fun nature opens up our minds making them more receptive.

Cartoons are often drawn with great economy of line. In just a few strokes of the pen, the artist is able to capture the essence of an idea, or in the case of a caricaturist, to observe and exaggerate the key features of the subject. A cartoon presents the cartoonists point of view so you see what the cartoonist would like you to see in a situation and the young man I met in the office supply store does exactly that!

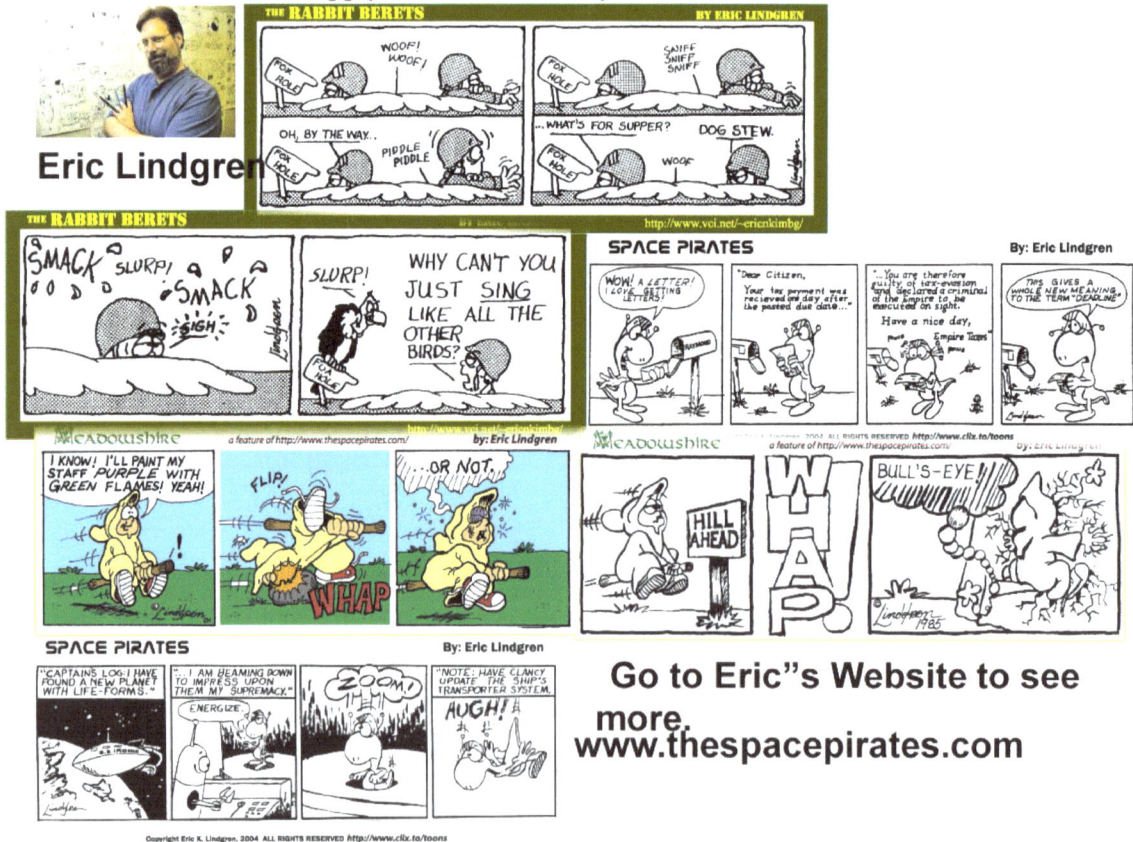

Eric Lindgren is a native of Orofino, Idaho and was born in 1962. He lives in Bowling Green, Kentucky, with my wife of 13 years and an ornery cat named Arthur.

When asked how he got into the art business of cartooning Eric said, "I learned to draw cartoons while in fourth grade. During high school I had a tendency to doodle in class. It was about 1978 or so when I first "doodled" Raymunde. Clancy followed about a couple of months behind."

When I asked Eric how he finally got to be living in Bowling Green, he said, "In about 1985 I attended WKU to become a technical Illustrator and while attending Western Kentucky University, the first "Space Pirates" strip was drawn. Raymunde found himself with not only Clancy, but the newly created C.L.A.I.R character as well. I let the trio loose in a self-published comic art paper that featured several other artists as also. "The Space Pirates" proved to be fairly popular. Not as popular as the "free door charge" coupons for some of the local bars that advertised in the same paper. The paper ran until 1989. 12 years later I got my first computer and went online. My internet service provider not only let me get online but also allowed be 10 megabytes of webpage space for a personal web space."

I asked when did the Space Pirates begin their circulation and Eric replied, ""The Space Pirates" went into circulation again and even gained more strips. In March, 2006 I also had other strips that I created online as well. I was taking a hiatus from "The Space Pirates" when the C.E.O. of Adventure Sports called one Sunday morning and asked if he could use Raymunde and the crew to help promote his youth line of products and activities. That request not only re-activated "The Space Pirates" but landed them their own official.com page as well."

Eric also does a comic strip called the "Rabbit Berets" and one called "Meadowshire"

Eric has recently allowed the "Space Pirates" to be used as a logo for the above mentioned company and he will do cartoons for company logos and merchandising. Just go to Eric's website www.thespacepirates.com to contact him.

The picture of Eric provided to us by Eric was taken by Joe Imel of the Bowling Green News and used by us with Eric's permission. All cartoons are copyrighted by Eric Lindgren.

Meet Kentucky artist Magdelene Appleby

One thinks of quilting as just sewing. However, there are a lot of artistic endeavors that go into the art of making a quilt. Quilts are regarded as significant

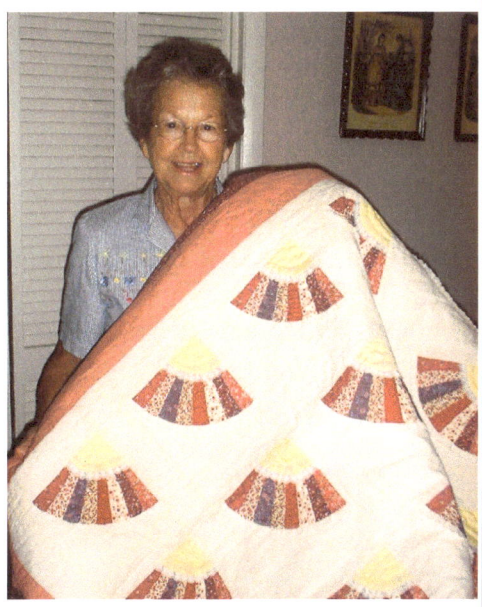
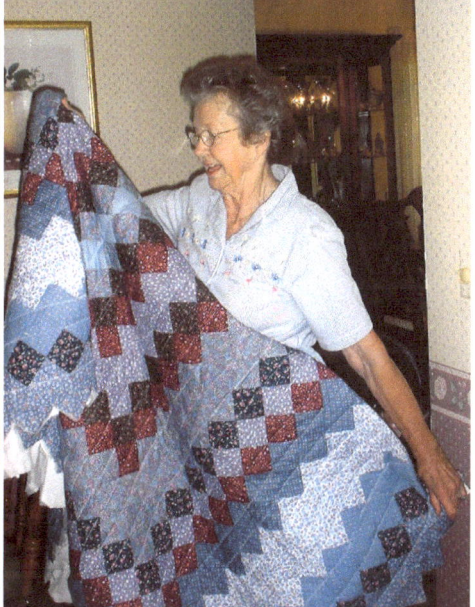

reflections of our country's history and are usually made to as a perfect gift for a special milestone in one's life such as a wedding or birth or anniversary. There are friendship quilts, Civil War Quilts, quilts using silks, ribbons and flannels, just to name a few.

Magdelene Appleby, a native of Hart County and a resident of Priceville, KY is an accomplished quilter and she knows all about quilts. When I asked her how many quilts she had done in her life time so far, she simply answered, "I can't remember, but there have been quite a few."

Her mother Cora Ash was a quilter and Magdelene started to make quilts with her grandmother, Julie Jones, using the long frames which one set up on saw horses. Now she uses snap frames which her husband always helps her put the quilts into.

When asked how long she had been quilting, she replied, "Over 40 years and all my quilts are hand sewn and hand quilted. My mother always had quilts going and she tacked lots of quilts. After my mother died I quilted all the quilts she had pieced."

Quilting seems to run in that family. Magdelene said when her grandson Jason was 4 years old he wanted to quilt and she gave him a needle, thread and thimble and he started quilting. Even though his stitches were quite long she says she left them in the quilt. He seemed really content to sew and watch TV. Her great granddaughter, Christina, who is 5 years old also, wants to help quilt.

Magdelene says, "When I went to how her show to thread a needle, she all ready knew how. She wanted to stick the needle up and down, but I had her threading my needle every time."

She went on to say her favorite quilts are the fan quilts and her girls and grandsons get the prettiest ones. She says it takes her over a month to do a quilt and she uses mainly natural fibers and cloth such as cotton.

She is currently working on a quilt with a pattern called "Trip around the World" which is shown on the right in the picture and the quilt on the left is her favorite quilt done in the Fan pattern.

There is much to the history of quilting, too much to discuss here. When the pioneers were preparing for the Overland Trail journey there was much preparation necessary before these families could begin their travels. Enterprising individuals were quick to publish guides to be sold to potential pioneers. Listed in these publications were the items one needed such as and including firearms, food for about 6 months and bedding including two or three blankets or comforters for each man, woman and child. It was suggested that each family should bring enough bedding to last a few years after arrival in the west; and it hinted that both quilting supplies and time on the part of the quilter would be scarce on the frontier. Clothing would be needed as well. As a result a great deal of pioneer sewing and quilting was done before the journey even began.

As the men talked eagerly of overcoming challenges and settling on the abundant rich farmland awaiting them the womenfolk were all too well aware of the dangers and hardships they would be facing and another reason that made pioneer women more reluctant about migrating west was their close ties with women friends and family. Most likely these dear friends would never see each other again. Thus friendship quilts were sometimes made for the woman leaving for westward lands. A friendship quilt served as a remembrance of dear ones left behind.

The women gathered together all the quilts, blankets and tied comforters they could either make or acquire. While very special quilts were packed in a trunk or used to wrap precious china, everyday quilts were left out for bedding. It wasn't long before women found this bedding to be necessary for many other uses. A folded quilt offered a little padding on the wagon seat for the person driving the oxen or any one riding over the long rough trail. When winds rose up and screamed across the dusty plains blankets, quilts and comforters were used to cover the cracks and any other openings that let the choking dust inside the wagon.

Our lives today do not carry those types of hardships. However, quilting has continued and it seems it will be handed down generation to generation through people like Kentucky Quilting Artist, Magdelene Appleby.

Meet Kentucky artists John Diebold and Bonnie Skees

The sign said, "We Know our Glass From a Hole-In-The-Ground!" and the store front was loaded with all kinds of beautiful stained glass pieces. I could not resist stopping by and finding out about the people that were inside Aardvark Art Glass, Inc. last week when I was over in Louisville since I am constantly learning that Kentucky abounds with talented artists.

Two such people are John Diebold and Bonnie Skees, stained glass artisans, partners and owners of Aardvark Art Glass, Inc.

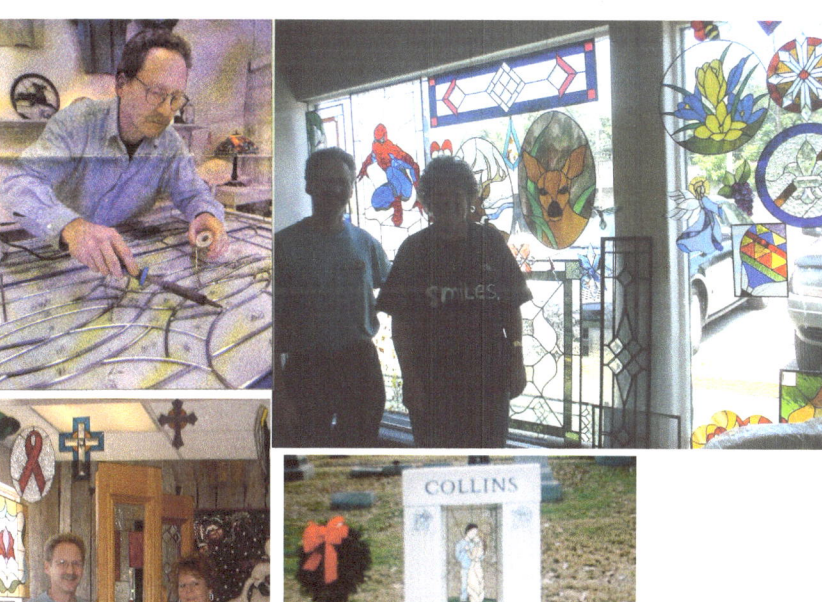

John Diebold & his partner Bonnie Skees in their studio/store in Louisville Aardvark Art Glass 3310 Preston Hwy.

John graduated as an art major from the University of Louisville in 1985, thus bringing with him a lot of artistic talent for pattern design. He says he never did any stained glass work, but when his parents were remodeling their home he saw his first piece of stained glass and loved what he saw. This caused him to become an apprentice at another studio.

Bonnie worked for 17 years with Anthem and she did stained glass as a hobby and after becoming quite good at it she started to teach night classes. It was during that time that she met John at the studio he was working at.

One thing led to another and they decided to open up their own studio in 2000. Bonnie said it took a lot of courage on her part to decide to leave a good paying day job of long standing to start out on her own with John in their new venture. Both of their spouses were supportive and help out when needed.

Bonnie likes the teaching end of the business best and John likes the art creativity and designing best, so it makes for a winning combination.

They give classes, sell supplies, do custom work and make repairs. However, they have created some interesting pieces that I had never seen before, such as stained glass memorial inserts for cemetery head stones or stained glass pieces with your pet's image in stained glass, plus it's photo inserted in part of it and the pet's name engraved on another part.

These two artists are easy to talk with and their humor comes across instantly. They have good communications with their customers whether they are long standing or with someone like me who just walked in out of curiosity. Their work is traditional yet original and of fine quality and you are instantly greeted with a smile.

So the next time you are in Louisville, stop in at Aardvark Art Glass, Inc. at 3310 Preston Hwy and meet stained glass artists John Diebold and Bonnie Skees because as they say, "We Know our Glass From a Hole-In-The-Ground!"

This week's Kentucky artist is Kellie Diamond

It is always a pleasure to meet people who live by design. One such person is Kellie Diamond who lives in Bonneville with her partner, Tim Brelig and their 3 year old sons Ari and 6 year old Max on their 114 acre farm, "Falling Springs Flowers" which they started in 1994.

Here in an extremely peaceful and serene setting she and Tim raise 1 ½ acres of flowers the bouquet and cut flower market in Louisville. It is also here that she raises two active and charming sons; helps build their home, raise their food, and tend flocks of goats, geese and ducks. A busy life, but one chosen by design!

It is also here that during the slowed down fall and winter months, Kellie gets to do what she loves. Paints!

Born in Cincinnati, Kellie Diamond has lived in Southern California, Minneapolis, Philadelphia and Newcastle Upon Tyne, England. These diverse travels, plus being fortunate to have a mother who was an art educator and artist, Kellie has been drawing and painting from a very young age.

Graduating from Swarthmore College with a Bachelors Degree in Art and Art History, she studied with Philadelphia artists Brian Meunier, Joyce Nagata and Randal Exon. She also spent 1 ½ years studying pottery win Minneapolis artist, John Heck. Pottery is her second love.

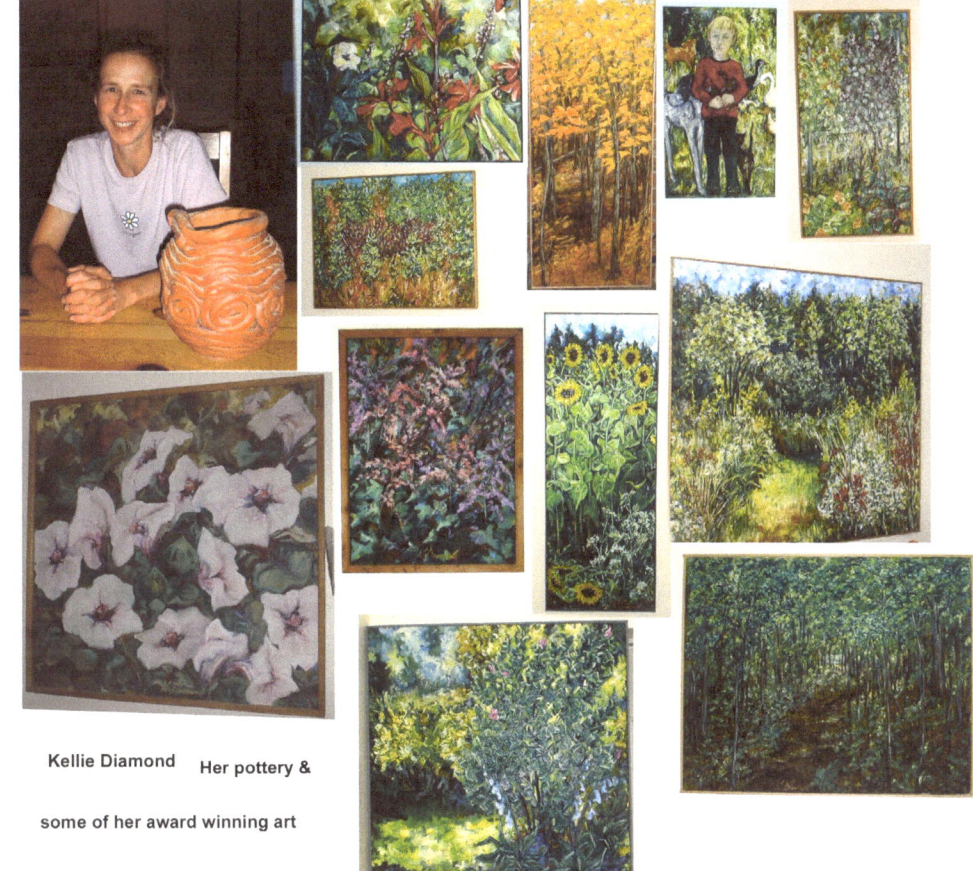

Kellie Diamond Her pottery &

some of her award winning art

Kellie says she has great love for both oil painting and pottery. She loves the tangibility and process of the clay when making pottery and the colors and broad strokes of oil when she does a painting. Since Kellie's life involves living close to the land and to nature, it is only natural that her paintings reflect the land and nature.

In 1998 Kellie was featured in an article in Glamour Magazine and her work has been shown in Minneapolis, Philadelphia and across Kentucky. She has received many awards and acclaim. Many of her paintings are in private collections throughout the USA.

Kellie Diamond may be reached at 270 524 8478 for appointments to view her art which is for sale at her studio.

Meet Kentucky artist J.C. Lively

It was like walking into the old west. The log cabin is nestled into a cool lovely bit of wooded acreage. Off to the side is the old blacksmithing building. The evening breeze softly moved the trees. It was quiet, with the exception of the trees nothing moved and it was hard to realize I was still in Kentucky. Matter of fact I was only over on Raider Hollow Rd. in Priceville.

I knocked at the door, nothing, peered into the darkness, not a sound, so it was quite normal to yell, "Hello the house!" Still nothing and as I turned to walk away, a small yellow haired sprite of a girl opened the door. This was Hanna, the next door neighbor of J.C. Lively, the craftsman I was looking for.

Hanna led me through the cool, darkened log cabin, saying that J.C. was down in the basement working. Her mother Sharon went to fetch J. C. They were over visiting making birdhouses that day.

At last the man himself emerged and I really felt I was in the old west. I got the feeling that J. C. Lively was a man born 100 years too late. He should have been in Montana, Wyoming or even Colorado. There is a strong, gentle quietness about him as he showed me all the things he makes.

J.C. told me he was the 4th or 5th generation to live on the land. He is a native of Hart County and he built his log home 36 years ago. It is a beautiful home. The kitchen is adorned with handy things that he hand forged in his blacksmith shop, as is the rest of his home.

He said he started doing this type of craft around 1986. He told me he has been a blacksmith, shoeing horses all his life. He says he does the hand forged items as a hobby only. However, he does have a website where one can go and see all the things he makes and then order them.
www.raiderhollowblacksmithshop.com

He, himself, admits that even though he loves where he lives, he yearns for the time when he can revisit Montana, Wyoming and Colorado. In 1977 he sold all his cows and went to Montana where he worked on guest ranches for 2 years. He worked at Guntown Mountain for 7-8 years and ran the blacksmith forge over there.

Still a blacksmith, though he has another day job, he enjoys his hobby of hand forging many items. His best seller is his personalized horseshoe where he will put your name on it. He makes gun racks, crane hoof picks, horse shoe belt buckles, horse shoe napkin holders, horse shoe rocking chairs, boot jacks, basket hangers, horse shoe cowboy figures, candle holders, horse shoe furniture, coat racks, stationary desk sets, horse shoe nail jewelry, branding irons, half moon pot racks, chuck wagon dinner bells, towel holders, cooking forks and fireplace iron sets, pot racks and heart shaped candle holders, just to name a few of the many things he is able to make.

He will personalize any of these items and he will do customize work. His prices are very reasonable and you can either go to his website of call him at 531 1451 for an appointment to see the things he makes.

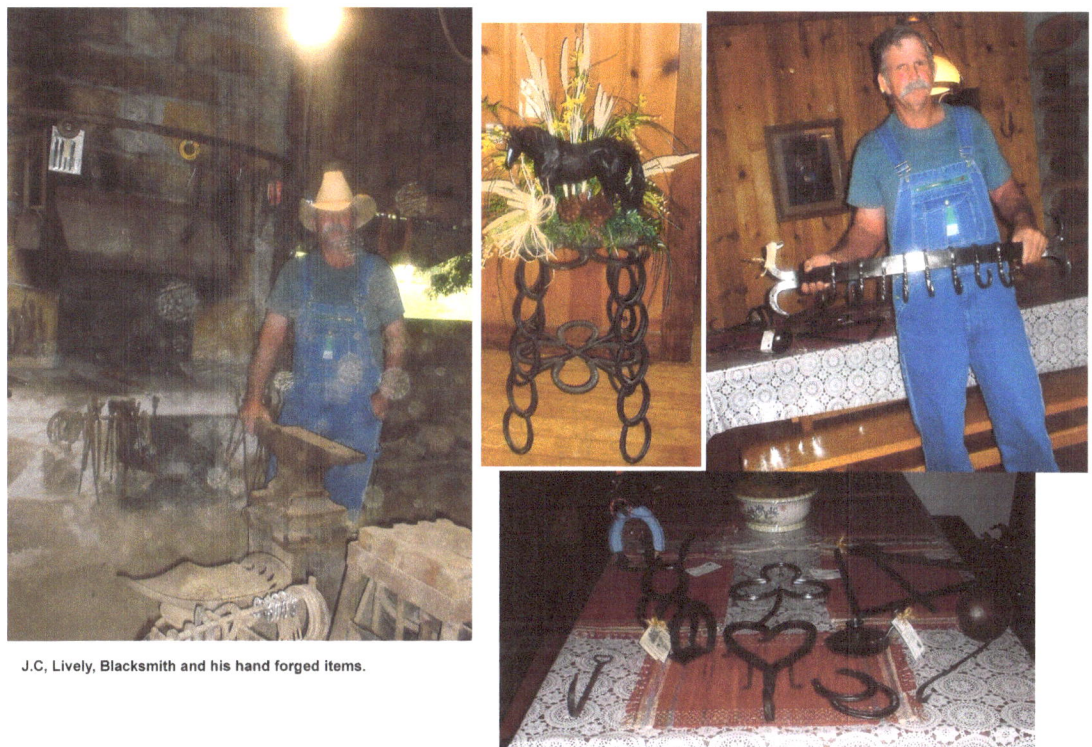

J.C, Lively, Blacksmith and his hand forged items.

Better go and see some of these things and have him make you something, before the call of the west sets in and J.C. heads out to the west he loves as much as Kentucky. If you are lucky he just may show you the knives he makes out old wagon springs with handles of deer, elk horn or wood.

Meet Kentucky artist Jane McTeigue

Jane McTeigue of 890 Gaddie Cemetery Rd. in Bonnieville is a visual artist specializing in book arts and paper engineering. Jane and I had been trying to arrange both our busy schedules to do this interview when we accidentally met at a mutual friend's 4th of July cookout.

We both took an instant liking to each other and we arranged for a meeting the next day. Jane a Native of New York, who was raised in Massachusetts, considers herself a nomad. She has lived in Sante Fe, New Mexico for 14 years, British Columbia Canada for a couple of years, has been to China, just to mention a few places and now makes her home in Bonnieville with her husband, Ken Neagle.

55

Jane's career in bookbinding began in 1987 when she was awarded a scholarship to study book arts at the Oregon School of Arts and Crafts in Portland. Since then Jane has worked with many book artists throughout the U.S., teaching, sharing ideas, and creating books of all shapes and sizes.

In 1992 Jane accepted a position as a pop-up book designer at White Heat Ltd. in Santa Fe, New Mexico, which at the time was one of the leading pop-up book designers in the world. Not only did this job offer her an inside view of the publishing, illustrating, printing, and book marketing industries (including traveling to China to oversee production and assembly), but it was at White Heat that Jane earned the title of Paper Engineer, designing 3D mechanics in dozens of books sold nationally and internationally.

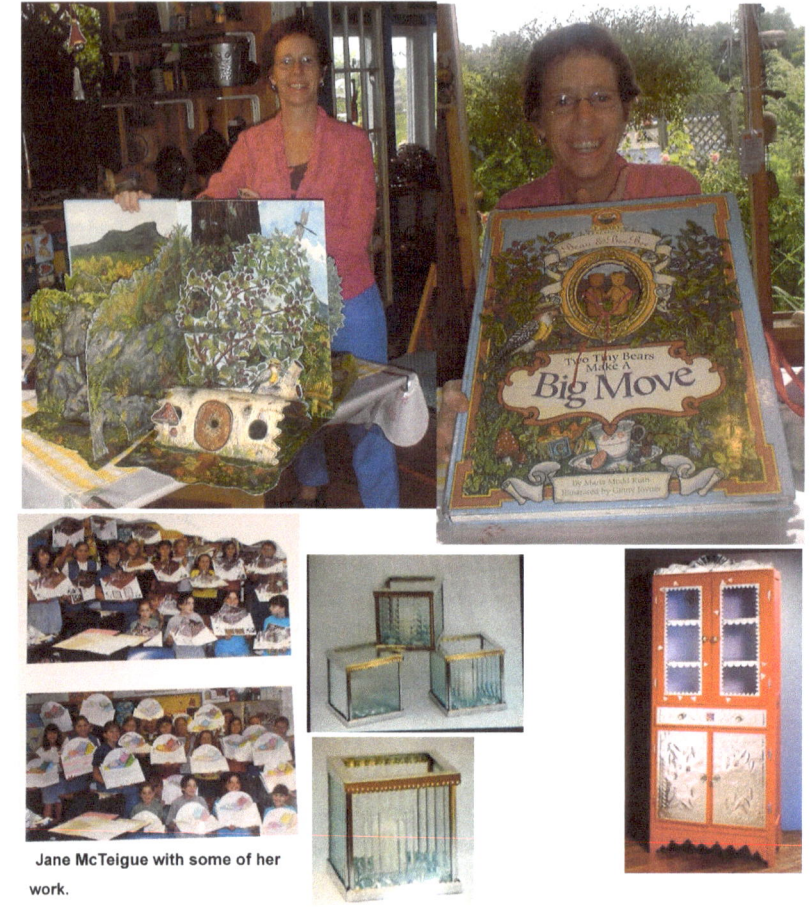

Jane McTeigue with some of her work.

Jane's pop-up books are a delight and she is an absolute genius in this field. She is a Kentucky Arts Council Roster Artist and since moving to Kentucky over 4 years ago has been busy teaching book arts in art centers and schools throughout the Commonwealth.

She currently goes to schools throughout KY for 5 to 10 days and teaches kids from K-12 how to make pop-up books. She says the grades 3-7 really get into them. Their subjects cover math, geometry, electricity, Kentucky history, you name it. So far Jane has helped 7,500 students create 7,500 pop-up books! Jane says she gets great joy out of the joy and excitement the kids get with the "pop-up book" lady as they call her. You can see the pictures of a class of kids with their pop-up books.

It is a lot of hard work to create these books. Jane says it takes about 2 years to make a commercial pop-up book which includes the creation of an idea, to making the prototype, to getting it onto the bookstore shelf!

The one big book you see her with is titled, "Beau and BeeBee, Two Tiny Bears that Make a Big Move". This is a very large book as you can see in proportion to Jane. She said the author needed a rush job and she was able to get the prototype completed in 9 months. A monumental job!

Along the way, Jane took up tinsmith working as a hobby. For many years she sold everything she could produce at art galleries in Sante Fe, New Mexico. She has also created custom orders for hotels and special customers. Her tin smith art is as small as a picture frame or as large as a cupboard. She even had her own small studio while living in Sante Fe.

This writer is amazed that Jane is so tremendously accomplished in both these fields and when talking with her, one gets the impression that she is able to do anything she puts her mind to. However, both these fields are her true loves and she is excellent in both. This writer had never been exposed to pop-up books except what I had bought for my children when they were younger. I never thought of how they were made, designed or whatever. They were just there in the store and until today I had never met a paper engineer before. However, I have seen a lot of tin smith work throughout my world travels and Jane's is the finest I have ever seen.

Jane is getting ready to put up her own website. However, in the meantime, one can reach her at janemcteigue@hotmail.com or call her at 270 531 1015 if you want to order a very special piece of tin ware or have her design an incredible cupboard, mirror, candle holder or towel holder for you or even have her design a pop-up book for all you KY authors out there. She's really, really busy, but if you are very, very lucky she may well be able to squeeze you in. Her work is worth every penny she commands!

Meet Kentucky artist Rachel Thompson

Rachel Thompson is a 15 year old cartoonist, a native of Hart County and Munfordville who is also a sophomore at Hart County High School.

She started to draw in the 8th grade and soon discovered she liked to draw the Japanese cartoons better than anything else. Rachel took 2 semesters of art in high school and has

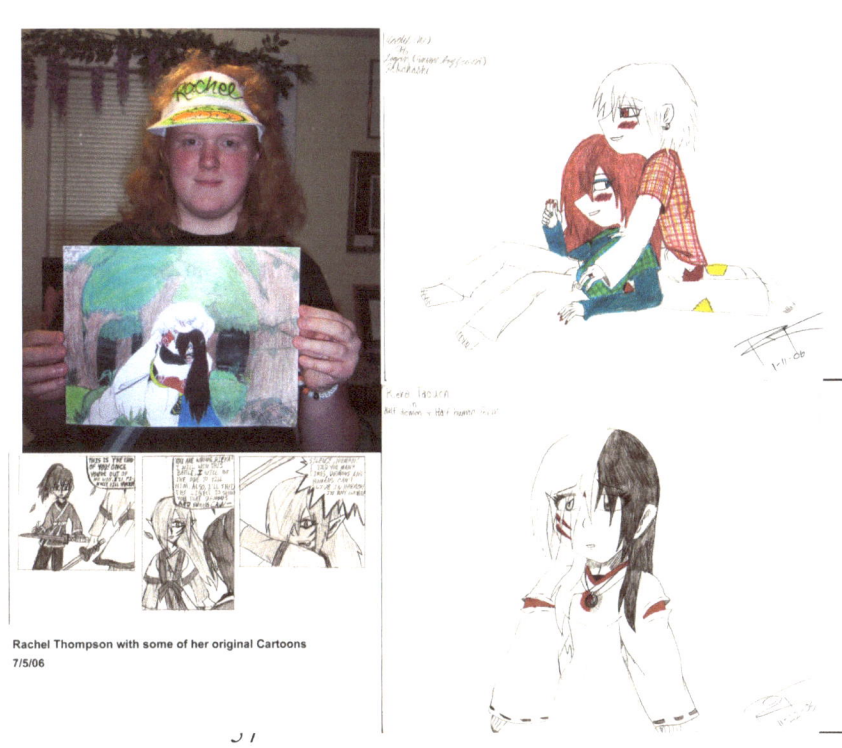

Rachel Thompson with some of her original Cartoons 7/5/06

developed at least 10 of her own characters.

She always tries to create her own storylines whether from imagination or inspiration. One of her goals is to create her own Manga which is a Japanese comic book which is read from right to left.

Manga (Pronounced *Mahn-ga*) is the Japanese word for comics and print cartoons. Outside of Japan, it usually refers specifically to Japanese comics. Manga developed from a mixture of *ukiyo-e* and foreign styles of drawing, and took its current form shortly after World War II. It comes mainly in black and white, except for the covers and sometimes the first few pages. Popular manga is often adapted into anime (Japanese for animation) once a market interest has been established. (Manga is sometimes mistakenly called "anime" even when not animated.) Adapted stories are often modified to appeal to a more mainstream market. Although not as common, original anime is sometimes adapted into manga (such as *Neon Genesis Evangelion* and *Cowboy Bebop*).

One of her characters is named Rieka Taouchi which is ½ human and ½ demon form and you can see her in one of Rachel's cartoons shown here.

Rachel is quite adept at creating this type of strip and though she knows quite a lot about it she realizes she has to learn a lot more including just the basics of art. She says one of the things she dislikes is drawing on demand, which is something most art courses teach in their lesson plan. She enjoys the spontaneous action of her story line cartoon characters.

For the past 4 or 5 years Rachel has enjoyed playing the clarinet in the Hart County High School band. She also loves to sing and does a lot of it in her church. Another one of her favorite pastimes is doing impersonations of cartoon characters.

In the future we need to keep our eyes open for this young artist as this writer feels she may achieve her artistic goals.

Meet Kentucky Artist William Roy White

I've seen a lot of stuff in 72 years. I am seldom in awe of anything anymore. However, I went to interview a fellow called William "Roy" White and I was blown away!

Let's just call this artist Roy as everyone else calls him. Roy lives in Munfordville with his lovely wife Sandra and his children and a 2 year old grandchild. A veteran of the US Army after 12+ years he now works in Tyson Bearings

Roy is a native of Buna Beacon-Buna Texas. As an East Texan he graduated from Buna Beacon High School and then went into the army in 1978. He met and married Sandra who is a Munfordville girl.

He started to draw while in Germany and his medium is colored pencils, occasionally going into oils. Roy has had no serious training and basically is self taught. While in the Army his talent attracted the "higher ups" and he was called upon to do murals and logos for the army including a reproduction of a Frank Frazetta work on a 20' x 20' rock for the Army.

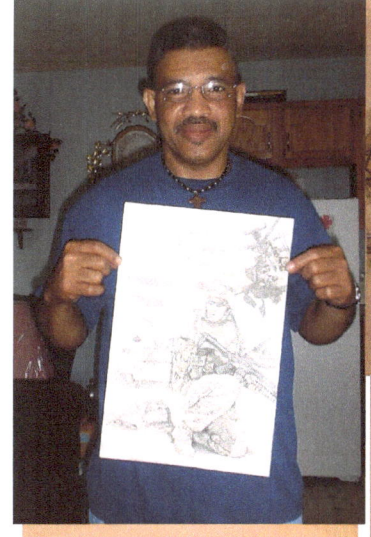

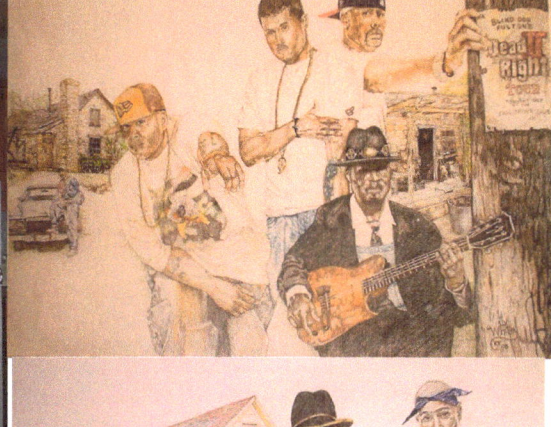

Roy is a quiet man who is motivated by his wife Sandra who truly believes in his art. This writer considers him a serious contender for the art world and Avalon Art Gallery of Munfordville has become his sole agent for his works.

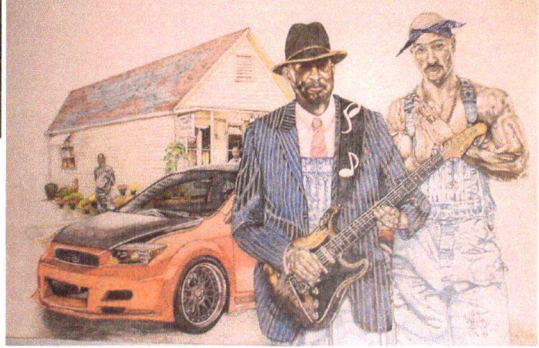

William Roy White

7/9/06

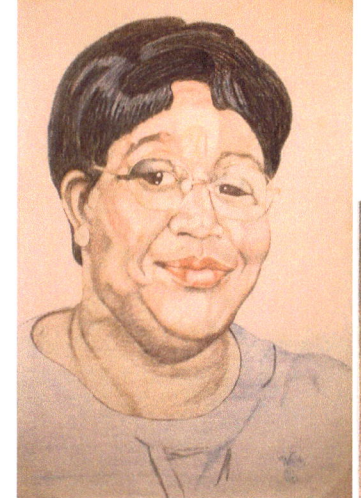

The works of William "Roy" White tells a story. Many of his subjects are black people and their beauty shines though his work.

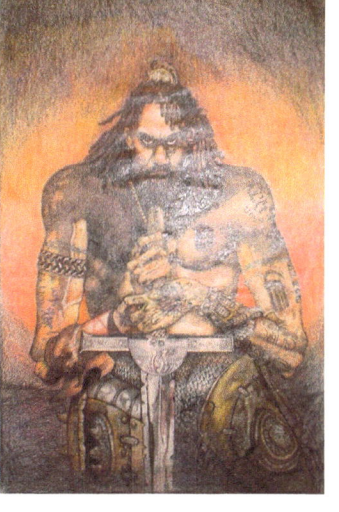

As a veteran and a military man, he paints what he knows. His drawings of the military are breathless. He has captured the essence of our military heroes, the "everyman" who left home to defend their country as shown in "Fire Fight", "Semper Fi" and "Over There". His painting titled "Highway 61" is of his father as a musician in Louisiana. His painting of Hart County Council Woman Alice Shirley, his aunt, captures her strength and energy.

The painting this writer loved is the one of his wife Sandra. This is 16 x 20" oil on canvas that is beyond words. It truly captures the essence of Sandra which is also the title of this painting. Another exciting work is called "Chittlin Circuit". He captures the essence of black musicians entirely.

Roy's works are now being offered at the beginning gallery price of $1,200.00 and he also offers signed Limited Edition prints framed and matted at $90.00 and can be seen on the web at http://www.learn-america.com/stories/storyReader$1780 or at Yessy Art Gallery at this site http://www.yessy.com/AvalonStudio/White.html?i=24539 Occasionally Roy moves into the world of fantasy as shown in his piece "Warrior".

The amazing thing about this artist is that he has never had an art lesson in his whole life. He just does it! Everything about his work is artistically correct. His pictures tell a story and it is told in incredible detail.

Roy also is a wood carver who carves beautiful walking sticks which he usually gives to people as gifts. Even these are beautifully done with incredible detail and colors.

This writer predicts that William "Roy" White is an upcoming black artist to be watched. His works are going places. Buy them now while you can! Appointments to view his work can be made by calling Avalon Art Gallery at 270 524 9567. Munfordville can look forward to being put on the art map by this artist's works.

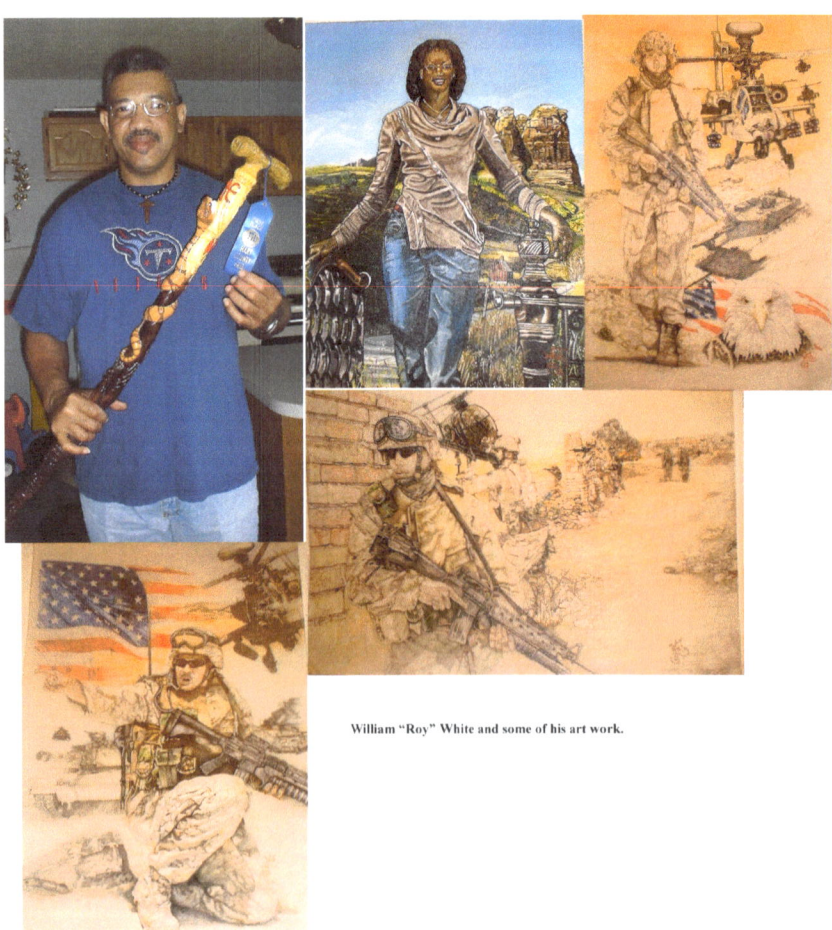

William "Roy" White and some of his art work.

Meet Kentucky artist Sharon Chartier Haines

Earlier this year I attended the Kentucky Market show over in Louisville and as I was awed by all the talent displaying their wares, I was especially delighted to see a booth called Natural Accents filled with beautiful (Natural/Organic) Cornshuck Flowers and Figures; Decorated Wreaths; Floral Swags; Centerpieces; Christmas Decorations & Ornaments all made by an artist and craftsperson named Sharon Chartier Haines.

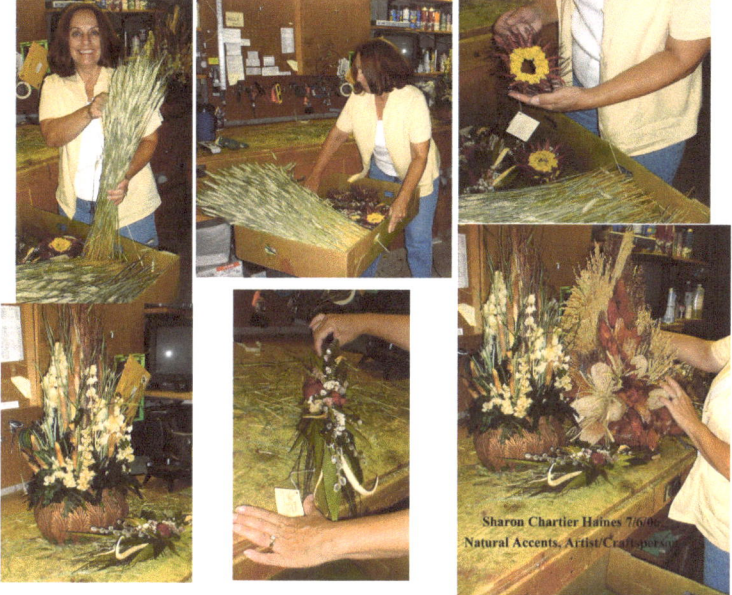

It took me awhile to get time to contact Sharon who only lives close by in Park City. Then it took us both some time to arrange our busy schedules to be able to do this interview. Sharon does about 15 shows a year throughout KY, IN, IL and OH. She is a juried presenter at everyone of these exhibits.

Well, I finally made it over to Sharon's studio in Park City where she lives with her husband who owns and operates 225 acres of farm land with 125 head of Black Angus cattle. This is a 3rd generation business.

Sharon is a native of Michigan and was a high school art teacher with degrees in Home Economics and Art. She spent 9 years teaching in those fields.

Q. How did you get started in your present endeavors?
A. I was asked to create a workshop for the Michigan County Extension in 1984 and it just grew from there.

Q. Do you use all natural material as your business name implies?
A. Yes. I grow 90% of it on 1 acre. I grow greens, grasses, pods, veggies, fruits, flowers, whatever I can dry. I even grow my own wheat. My husband drills it in for me. The other 10% I buy and that usually just comprises the wreath bases or I would never get anything done. However, I do make the grapevine wreaths as I grow the grapevines on a fence and they are cuttings from my grandmother's grapevines at her home. I even grow the gourds I use.

Q. What are some of the things you grow?
A. I grow lavender, yarrow, wheat. I grow many different things each year. Different Millets, I have 4 different varieties of Pussy Willows. I grow okra, 100 different pepper

plants and I never eat one of them. I grow a whole range of statice, cockscomb, bells of Ireland. My husband laughs. He spends all his time tearing out teasel and I grow it.

Q. Do you classify this just as a hobby?
A. No! This is a definite artform put together with the mind of a pallette and it starts in my garden when I decide what to plant. Then it goes from there. It helps to have been an art major because I see my final product as a completed work of art since no two pieces are every exactly alike.

Q. How hard is it doing all those exhibitions and shows a year?
A. It is quite hard and time consuming. I drive to each one and each one is a "one of a kind" exhibit. All the shows are juried, so all my work must be juried. Each show is a two day show and there is the setting up before hand and taking down. There is a lot to bring and each item has to be handled carefully.

Q. Do you belong to any guilds or art societies?
A. Yes, I am a member of the KY Guild of Artists and Craftsman. I was the VP for 1 year and the President for 2 years. I was also on the standards committee for 4 years and then set up the juried committee for the KY Craft Marketing Program. I also belong to the Louisville Artisans Guild.

Sharon took me down into her "dungeon", which is her large basement studio and I was astounded by the scope of what she does down there. From floor to ceiling, racks filled with boxes of dried items she uses to make her beautiful arrangements.

She went on to tell me that the process is quite detailed. She uses glycerine to dry her items. However, glycerine causes a loss of clorophyll (green), so she must put the colors back in with a natural commercial dye.

Q. Do you do custom work?
A. Oh yes. People often bring me containers of all sorts that have special meanings and memories for them and I fill them with all kinds of dried things that create a long lasting home decoration for them.

When you want something really special made just for you give Sharon a call. Her work is beautiful and her prices are really reasonable. The name of her business is Natural Accents and the artist is Sharon Chartier Haines of 5294 Pk City-Glasgow Rd Park City, KY 42160 you may call (270) 749-8862 or email her at *kshaines@alltel.net* Her studio hours are by appointment only.

Meet Kentucky artist Penny Boeckmann

Her favorite saying is "Life expands and contracts in direct relationship to what courage you have" and Horse Cave artist Penny Boeckmann proves it in her many pieces of artistic work.

Penny, a native of Horse Cave and Hart County works at the Caverna Board of Education as their finance officer and she has been there for 10 years. When not working hard at her "day job" she spends much of her spare time creating the most incredible works of arts and crafts.

Penny lives with her charming dog Grace who really doesn't know she is a dog in a wonderful home filled with many pieces of her work. She says she has always been drawing and painting, even as a child. She even had private lessons in Glasgow as a young girl. During the 10 years she lived, attended college and worked in Nashville, TN she took many night art classes and she currently will start up again in the fall with art classes in Bowling Green, KY.

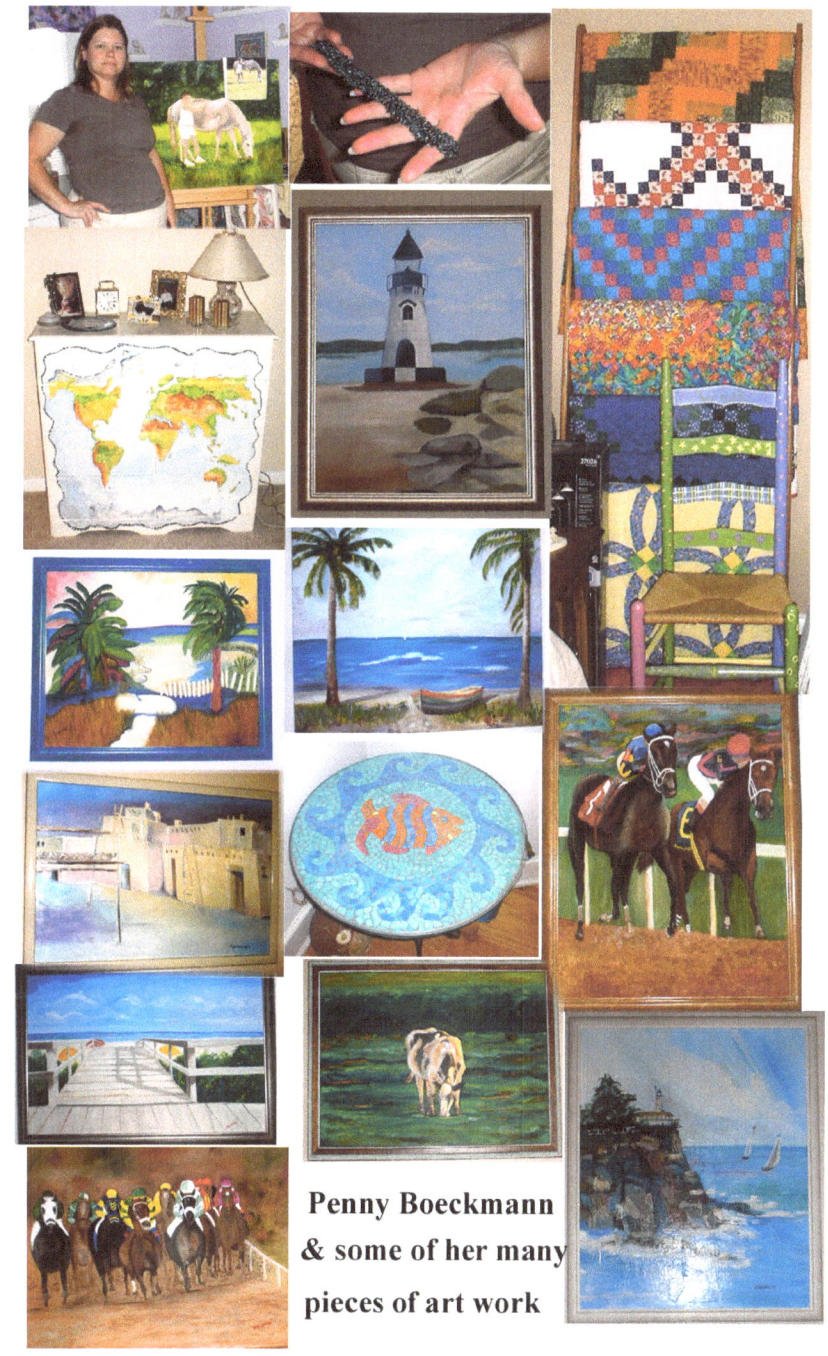

Penny Boeckmann & some of her many pieces of art work

Though she has tried other mediums, her love of oils is where she spends most of her time. Like many artists she goes through phases of subjects, i.e. light houses, cows, horses, but she keeps coming back to landscapes. She is shown next to her current commission project of a girl and her horse.

Penny knows no bounds. Anytime she sees something she says to herself, "I can do that!" She then proceeds to figure it out and does it as in the line of lovely beaded bracelets and necklaces she creates of tiny, intricate beads of shimmering colors and designs similar to the ones that are found in the most expensive shops.

She showed me some of her hats and scarves she knits and these are the kind of things filled with whimsical textures and colors, the kind of fun apparel that would be found in the most upscale boutiques!

Penny also makes amazing quilts which she learned when she took a course on quilt making and in her talented hands; the least unappealing, mundane piece of wood furniture is turned into the most charming fun filled piece of art furniture that would also be found in some of the upscale shops in the more worldly parts of the globe.

This artist loves life, loves to travel whenever she can and what she sees and absorbs in her travels shows in her work.

Penny does custom work for people and you can call her at 786 1328 for an appointment to have her make something individually for you.

Meet Kentucky artist Carl Correll

3-D art never gets all the attention it deserves. It is mostly lumped into the crafts division. However, even crafters need to have an artistic eye and this week's artist; Carl Correll indeed has an artistic eye.

Originally he was a hobbyist oil painter, working on large canvases and usually with a pallet knife. Many of his paintings still reside in many New Yorker's homes as that is where most of his art work sold. Now and then one will find one in Florida when one of the owners retires there and takes the painting along.

At one time he decided to take up welding and created incredible weather vanes

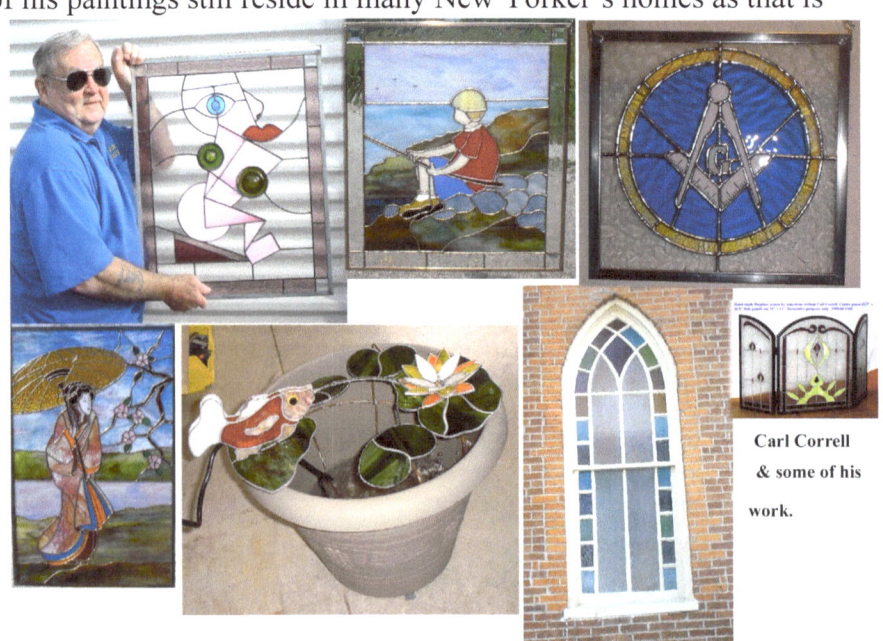

Carl Correll & some of his work.

using the purchaser's favorite theme as the design. A few years later he decided to create large copper garden helixes that twirled in the wind. He designed and created all kinds, 6 foot high ones, hanging ones; you name it he made them. A few can still be seen outside his studio today. However, the art and creation of stained glass projects has become his one true love.

Carl is a native of Scranton, PA and lived in New York from the time he was 6 until 1979. During that time he has lived in various places such as Hawaii and Japan. From 1979 until 1992 he lived in Florida and then after awhile to TN where he designed, built and operated a successful B & B, Campgrounds and Hostel for 6 years and now lives in Munfordville, KY where he operates Avalon Stained Glass School.

In amongst all that activity Carl decided to learn another hobby. The art of stained glass and before he knew it this subject basically took over his life. Though he knows the lead came method and has made many pieces, he enjoys the copper foil method best. He did both methods for many years before he decided to open Avalon Stained Glass School in March of 2005.

Prior to opening up the school he just quietly made windows, panels, and all kinds of things in stained glass which he either sold over the internet or to customers who found him and commissioned his work. During that time he continually heard from his customers that they wished they could do something as beautiful as the pieces he had made for them. Carl then decided that he would teach those who wished to learn, how easy and simple it was to make these works of art.

Since he has opened Avalon Stained Glass School he has taught many people how simple, easy and enjoyable it is to make these lovely pieces of art. Most of his students go on to have life long hobbies and a couple of graduates have opened up their own studios. He has even created an "Art for Youth" program whereby he teaches teens, ages 13 to 18, within 3 hours, all the steps of making 2 small stained glass projects, for only $49.00!

As an excellent and patient instructor he easily can impart his artistic talents to the student, thus allowing them to discover, usually to their own amazement, their own artistic abilities. He has designed his school to be a friendly and easy atmosphere to work in and he has also designed easy flexible prices (which start as low as $35.00) and hours to allow the students to fit it into their budgets and working schedules.

Between classes, Carl continues to work on his own artistic projects, commission work, or repairs and he himself is continually learning new techniques in this field. Plus he offers an extremely large supply of stained glass, supplies, and equipment for this area. He also offers glass etching and engraving. His latest project was creating a course for immortalizing your child or grandchild in stained glass. He just finished one of one of his grandchildren. He loves to create one of a kind stained glass art pieces such as his "Picasso in Stained Glass". He makes stained glass fire place screens, professional logos such as Realtor© logos, Masonic Logos, water fountains, spinning garden wind dancers and traditional fan arches, windows and panels.

Carl is a juried member of the South Central KY Arts & Crafts Guild and is a Member of KHAT (Kentucky Arts Heritage Trail). He is also a certified member of EBSQ and all his work comes with an ESBQ certificate of authenticity. He is member of KAHT (Kentucky Art Heritage Trail) He is also the only stained glass artist to be accepted into the 26th annual All Kentucky Fine Arts Exhibition and is the winner of the Bowling Green Women's Club Merit Award.

He loves to give free demonstrations to anyone who wishes to visit him during his open hours which are Tuesday thru Friday, 9 am to 5 pm and Saturday 8 am to noon, CT. Come and see him at Avalon Stained Glass School, Studio and Art Gallery at 100 Dave Wintsch Rd., Munfordville, KY 42765 (270) 524 9567. His work can be seen at his website which is www.learn-america.com   Carl says come in for a free demonstration.

Meet Kentucky artist Kate Kenny

We all pass her art at least once a day. Several of us pass it several times a day. It is rarely framed and we usually don't even notice it. Matter of fact we take it for granted. It is just there.

Who thinks a sign painter or a sign creator is an artist? Most of us do not.

Chester Harding an artist in the early 19th-Century countryside started out as a sign painter as did the likes of P. C. Leyendecker, Andrew Loomis and Norman Rockwell. A remarkably high percentage of fine artists have come out of sign shops, advertising agencies and printing establishments. These artists had what I call "the worker's edge." Sign painters showed up for work in the morning and painted all day. Steady work habits in the shop made it easier when they moved into their studios. Think of those huge hand-painted movie marquees that were produced in every town and city in the twenties and thirties--colorful, often highly competent, with great likenesses and an understanding of anatomy and chiaroscuro, to say nothing of lettering. And those guys were paid by the hour.

Unfortunately sign painting with a brush is a dying art and there will soon be no one left from whom one can learn the art of brush holding, esoteric brushes, mahl sticks, striper wheels, quills, pounce wheels and pounces, bridges, chalk-snaps, hook and ladder, projectors, grids, cut-awls, the list goes on and on. The need for speed and economy in show-card, billboard and other illustrative forms influenced and freshened does not allow Kate to sit down to work.

To get a good downward stroke or a nicely curved "S" takes more of the body than just a forearm. Pinstripers use their entire body. Sign shops do not have chairs for working. Chairs slow down production and one will not see a chair except at Kate's computer where she allows customers to see for them selves the designs she artistically creates in her mind.

Those of us who know Kate Kenny can identify with the handle of the "Mad-sign-tist" she gave herself a long time ago. Yet the "mad" part can usually be aptly applied to all of us artists and especially those of us who really call ourselves "painters". Also one would have to be slightly "mad" to deal with all the pressure customers put on sign painters, especially today. I can hardly imagine that kind of pressure being put on me when I decide to sit down and do a commissioned piece of art, yet it is there for sign painters. I have seen Kate there in her studio at the weirdest hours working away, hand painting signs that could not be done with the vinyl lettering that is often used today. Just laying out the designs or artistic illustrations would lay most of us low.

Kate is a painter! Just really look at her work. It is on our town signs, our business signs, our cars, fire trucks, etc. Wherever you look there it is! Her output is tremendous and like most of us new age painters she has many of the "bells and whistles" in her shop that allows her, Marty her husband, Savannah and Luke, their children who work there when school is out, plus her staff to get all our jobs done. Not only done, but done well, fast and artistically correct.

Her latest mural in Cave City is about 12 feet high and 25 ft long and was completely done by hand. A fine piece of artwork! Her signs for the KY Repertory Theater are pure works of art as far as I am concerned. Most of Kate's work out in California, done many years ago, still stands today, beautifully done, part of the local landscape and heritage that are like old master's works of art.

Kate and her family live in Munfordville off Rowletts Road with cats, dogs, horses, goats, chickens, turkeys, guinea hens and who knows what else. Besides all the things she and her family do to put "beans on the table", they find time to be good neighbors, do tons of civic things, participate in community activities, care for their place, garden, harvest and preserve their harvest and be a loving family. Whoever drops by, no matter when, is always welcomed with an offer of hospitality.

Kate even has time for a hobby which is stained glass making and she makes amazing panels which can be seen at their place of business.

So the next time you decide to walk into Kenny's Signs, Graphics & Awnings remember you are really walking into one of Kentucky's best artist's studio and you will be talking to one wild and talented creative artist.

Meet Kentucky artist Jana John

Who's the woman behind the mask? It is none other than the gifted clay artist Jana John of Louisville, KY and she specializes in whimsical masks and other pieces with a cat or woman theme.

Jana works out of her studio at home, where she hand-builds pottery, both decorative and functional, using terra cotta clay. She rolls out slabs of clay with a rolling pin and cuts out shapes freehand.

Her signature pieces have a delightful cat motif. She makes cat-shaped masks, platters, bowls, spoon rests and pins. This cat preoccupation comes from her love of cats.

Jana says, "I find cats have a lot of personality, which I try to capture in my designs," and she hopes they make you smile and they usually do.

She says, "The other masks belong to the "My Women" series. The are inspired by women I know, women I'd like to know, women I'd like to be, women I hope I'm not, in essences... all women!" Her wonderful "Bar Babes" are an integral part of this series. . The Bar Babes are women holding drinks -- martinis, margaritas or wine -- and wearing red high heels or red high-top sneakers. The Babes also appear on pins and spoon rests.

I met Jana last year when I discovered that she, along with me, was one of the 6 Kentucky artists chosen to do a 6 month doll creating project called "Journey Jots".

Jana John is a native of Oklahoma and has worked at newspapers in Oklahoma, Arkansas, Texas, Louisiana, Mississippi and Kentucky. In January 2000, Jana moved to Louisville, Ky., from Jackson, Miss., where she had lived since 1983. She and her husband, Butch John, have been in the newspaper business for the past 28 years. The rest of her family includes her cats — Yowzer and Munch.

Jana is a juried member of the Craftsmen's Guild of Mississippi Inc., the Louisville Artisans Guild, the Kentucky Guild of Artists and Craftsmen and the Kentucky Craft Marketing Program.

Besides being charming and functional her whimsical and vividly colorful cat platters and bowls are food-safe and dishwasher safe. The cat-shaped spoon rests can also serve as soap dishes or can hold your kitchen sponge or jewelry. Each is approximately 5 inches by 3.5 inches.

Jana says, "I'll be 51 on Sept. 28. I don't mind telling my age. I'm happy to have made it this far."

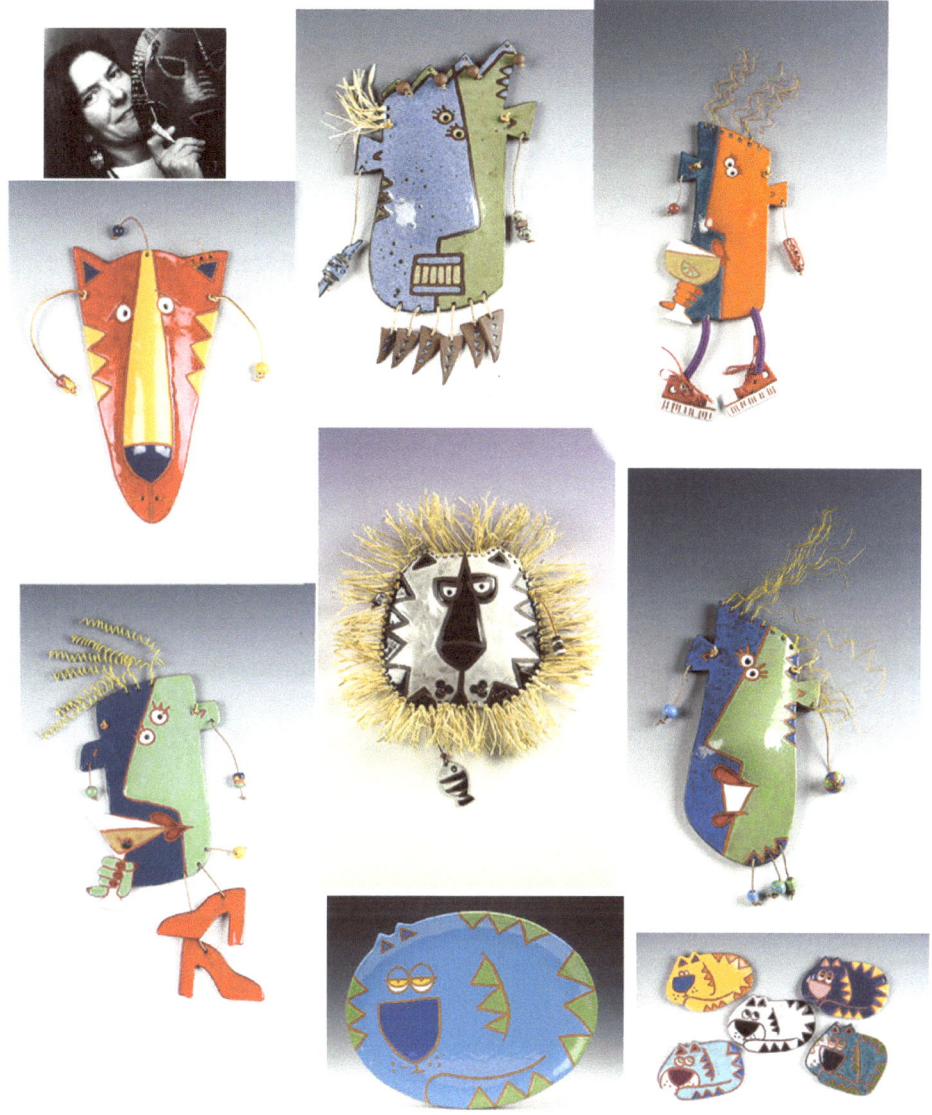

Jana also does special commission work and would be delighted to have you call her to have her make you anything special for your kitchen, home or garden. Her cell is (502) 271-9428. Home is (502) 479-8063. Work is (502) 582-7020.

In June of this year, Jana and five other artists opened an art gallery, called "Gallery Janjobe", in Louisville. The artist/owners sell their own work and the work of other artists on consignment. The gallery is located in the Mellwood Arts & Entertainment Center, 1860 Mellwood Ave. The center is the old Fischer meatpacking plant, which is being renovated and turned into artists' studios and spaces for galleries, cafes, an art supply store and more.

The gallery has been open since its Sneak Preview on June 30, but it will have its official Grand Opening on Friday evening, Sept. 29, and all day Saturday, Sept. 30. For information, call 502-899-9293.

Meet Kentucky artist James Pucket

James Pucket, a native of Hart County, was a farm boy, from a family of 9, raised up in Kessinger, KY. As a small boy he started sketching when he was about 9 or 10 years old taking lessons from a local neighbor artist who was a deaf mute. The artist was also tattoo artist who would give James pencil and paper to keep him occupied. Not only did he learn a lot of art from this man, but he learned the art of signing which he also used later on in his adult life. He was fortunate to have a teacher named Ora Logsdon in the one room school he attended in his youth, who encouraged his artistic leanings. Basically, James is a self taught artist.

James left home when he was about 18 years old and headed to Louisville where he lived for many years doing a variety of jobs. He started in a box factory, went on to selling life insurance, and then worked in American Air Filter. He left that to work as a teacher of signing and printing to deaf students. After a while he went back to American Air Filter where he worked until he finally retired from there.

During his working years and especially between jobs he managed to have his art support him and his family for awhile by taking 8 of his paintings and creating a series of signed limited edition prints of 2,500 each which he eventually sold out. Three of these were the wonderful pencil drawings he did of the L & M Foot Bridge in Louisville, The Lincoln Heritage House in Elizabethtown, and the old Churchill Downs.

James has quite a scrape book of awards and letters of recognition pertaining to his art work including a letter from Princess Anne and Lord Snowdon thanking him for one of his prints of the old Churchill Downs. He has won several KY state fair awards and has received recognition by the KY Historical Events Celebration Commission.

Though he has done watercolors and pastels, James says his favorite medium has always been oils. Earlier on he liked to paint birds and other wildlife, but as he has gotten older he says his eyes are not good enough for the fine details of feathers and fur, he stays with landscapes.

Over the years, James has created incredible pictures in his mind of the things he has observed and seen driving back and forth to work and these images become the subjects for his paintings.

He says the most unusual painting he ever did was for a lady who wanted a picture of her late dog painted on a tombstone.

After retirement, James came back to Hart County and now lives in Hardyville with wife Sylvia who is a native of Munfordville. Both met at their church after the passing of their respective mates.

James still paints and he frames his own paintings. Not only does he frame them himself, he builds the frames! Occasionally, he will do a commission job and he can be reached at 528 5640.

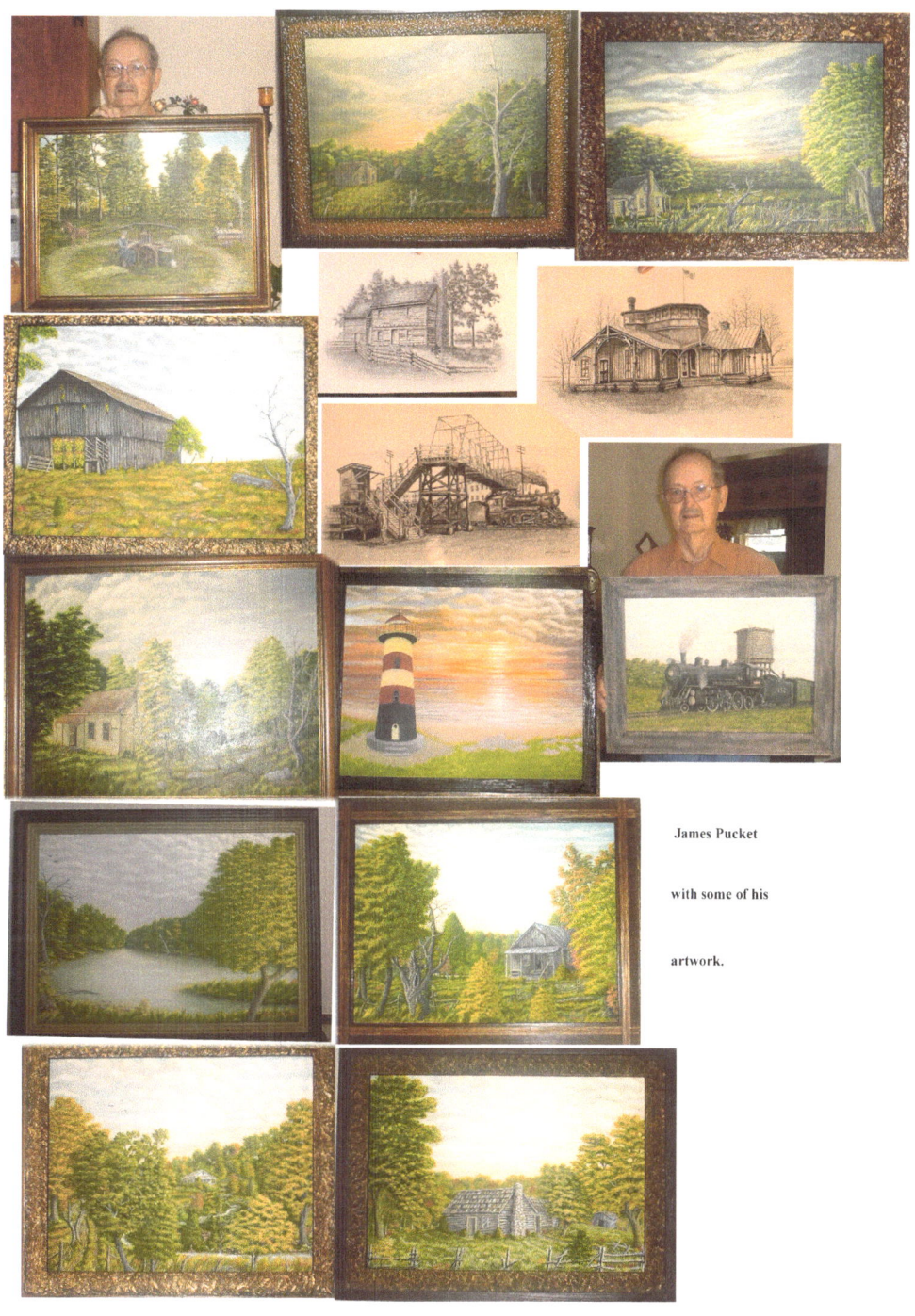

James Pucket

with some of his

artwork.

Meet Kentucky artist Patricia Griffin

Who would have thought being told as a child "not to touch" would bring Patricia Griffin into the world of perpetuating the ancient art of china painting?   Patricia, a native of

Michigan, has lived in Hart County and Munfordville since 1998 where she and her husband Dale raise Quarter Horses.

She can remember, as a small child, visiting a neighbor's home and seeing beautiful hand painted china. "Don't Touch" she was admonished! Yet she remembers she dearly wanted to touch it as it was so beautiful and she was an artistic child. The smell of clove oil, which is used in china painting, stayed with her for a long time.

As Patricia grew into adulthood, her talents

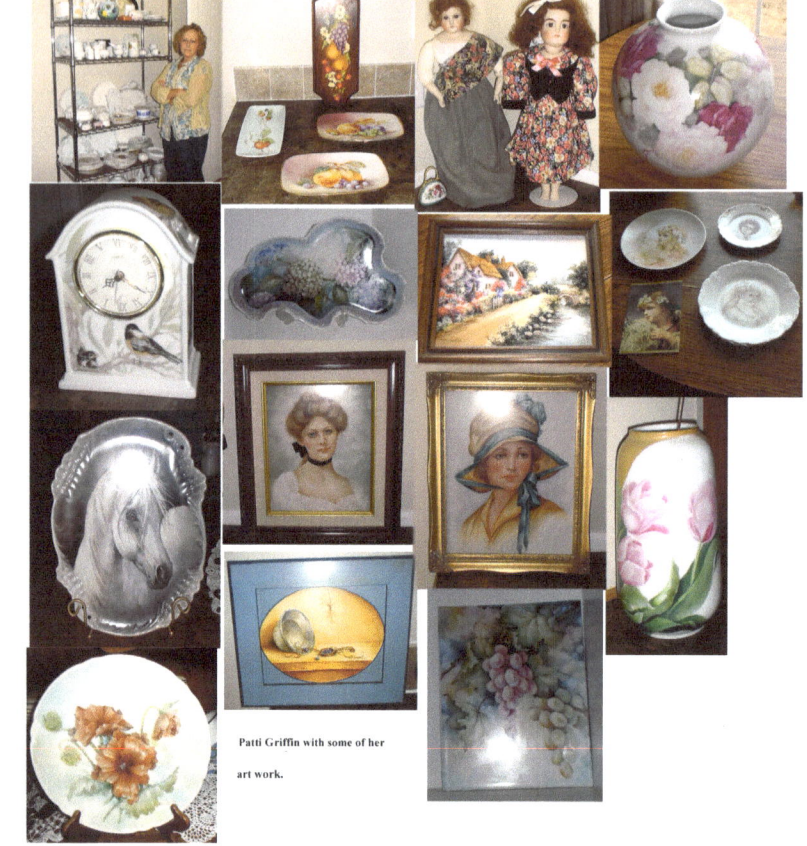

Patti Griffin with some of her art work.

brought her into the business of teaching people to paint. About 1975 she worked for a business and there she taught oil painting, decorative tole painting and doll painting and making.

Always remembering the smell of clove oil, she starts taking intensive courses and seminars about 1985. She searched for knowledge of china painting and even drove a 180 mile round trip once a week for 8 years to learn this ancient art.

Though called China painting, basically what Patricia does is Porcelain painting and there are three main kinds of porcelain: (1) hard-paste porcelain, (2) soft-paste porcelain, and (3) bone china. The differences between these types of porcelain are based on the material from which they are made. This material is called the body or paste.

Patricia buys her porcelain or china in a finished form, i.e. tea pots, cups, tiles, plates that are ready to be painted and fired in her kiln. She stocks everything anyone will need to get into this type of hobby. Can you just imagine creating your own set of hand painted china? Patricia showed me incredible vases, tiles, dishes, tea pots, you name it and each piece was more exquisite than the last. It was all beautiful!

Painting the porcelain surface may be done in several ways. One method is to use a colored glaze, such as the famous Chinese celadon. This glaze is a soft gray-green color. Another type of decoration is under glaze (designs painted on a piece before it is glazed). A deep blue made from the metal cobalt is the most dependable color used for under glazing. Cobalt blue has been widely used both in China and in Europe.

Paints that are applied over the glaze are commonly called enamels. A large variety of enamel colors were perfected at an early period. Most of them are made from metallic oxides, such as iron, copper, and manganese. Enamel colors require a second firing to make them permanent.

Porcelain painting in Europe differed greatly from porcelain painting in China. Chinese decorators separated each color from the next with a dark outline, but European artists blended colors together with no separating line. In addition, Europeans used decorations purely for their artistic value, but Chinese decorations were symbolic. For example, a pomegranate design symbolized a wish for many offspring because a pomegranate has many seeds.

Porcelain painting must be fired in a kiln to preserve and intensify its colors. This type of art is a slow but rewarding process. To paint a portrait on a piece of china is the most challenging of all work, but when one captures the likeness there is great joy in the finished product. Patricia says she starts most of her students off painting flowers as they can relate to that.

Depth of color is achieved by applying a layer and firing it in a kiln and then building up your layers until you get the result you want. Patricia says one does not need to be able to draw to be able to paint on china.   Patience and careful observation provides a good work for doing this type of art.

Patricia is quite knowledgeable about all this and has been teaching this ancient technique for many years. Her work is exquisite and truly has a look of days gone by. She has won many awards including some at our KY state fair and is a member of many societies including the World Organization of China Painters, a non-profit organization dedicated to the preservation of the art of hand painted porcelain which was started by Pauline Salyer in 1962 and finally officially founded by her in 1967. In 1977, the first World Wide Convention of the Organization was held in Oklahoma City, bringing together hundreds of artists from across the world. Today this organization has over 7,500 members.

She is also a member of IPAT (International Porcelain Artists and Teachers Inc.), Belles of Louisville and is the current President of the Lincoln Heritage China Painters in Elizabethtown.

Patricia says this is a very old art and similar to watercolor painting that was something that "ladies" did many years ago as a dainty art such as needlepoint. It also was a piece meal job for women in the 1800's who painted china, packed it up, sent it to Chicago for firing, received it back for further painting and when finished returned it for the few pennies they earned and it was considered their "pin" money.

Patricia says there are not many teachers in this field. Many of them are in their 80's and though this might seem like a lost art that is on the way out, my research shows that there are many people involved in this serious type of art throughout the world.

Patricia told me the thing she likes best about this is that she can get truly lost in working on it and all the stress and cares of every day life just goes by the wayside. She also enjoys teaching others how simple this is to do.
Patricia teaches at her home studio in Munfordville at 6783 Hwy 357 No. and she is about 7 miles from the Munfordville Courthouse. You may call her at 524 3267 for class hours. Her rates are extremely reasonable being only $9.00 for 3 hours of lessons. Patricia says one usually has a start up cost of approximately $30.00 and in about 6 weeks time they might have invested a total of $70.00. However, she says that will usually include enough to do their next piece. You do not need to invest in a kiln as your lessons include the firing.

Well, Pat, I'm convinced and I am going to become one of your students and this will become one of my winter projects. Who knows where it will lead me?

Meet Kentucky artist Sandy Novosel

Sandy Novosel is a native of Cleveland, Ohio, currently living in Glasgow, KY, who moved to Barren County 33 years ago when her husband took a job there.

She is a graduate of Cleveland Institute of Art and Western Reserve University with a Masters degree of Arts in Art. As an art teacher she only taught in the public school system for a year, but did a lot of substitute teaching in the high school systems as she raised her family.

Sandy said she is a disaster in oil painting and her love of watercolors compensates for that. She loves the surprises and lack of control that she gets in her watercolor painting.

She has been a weaver, a potter, and a rug braider over the years. However, her one true love is her water color painting as one can see in her works of art. Sandy says she paints solely for herself even though she sells her paintings. Her art prices are very reasonable at ¼ sheets being $100.00 and up and ½ sheets being $250.00 to $300.00 each. This year she had 2 shows in Bowling Green, KY and 1 show in Glasgow, KY.

As an avid gardener she loves to paint flowers and fruits. Her advice to anyone who wants to paint is that you should be prepared to enter into another world because you begin on a new adventure. For Sandy, a blank sheet of paper is the beginning of a journey.

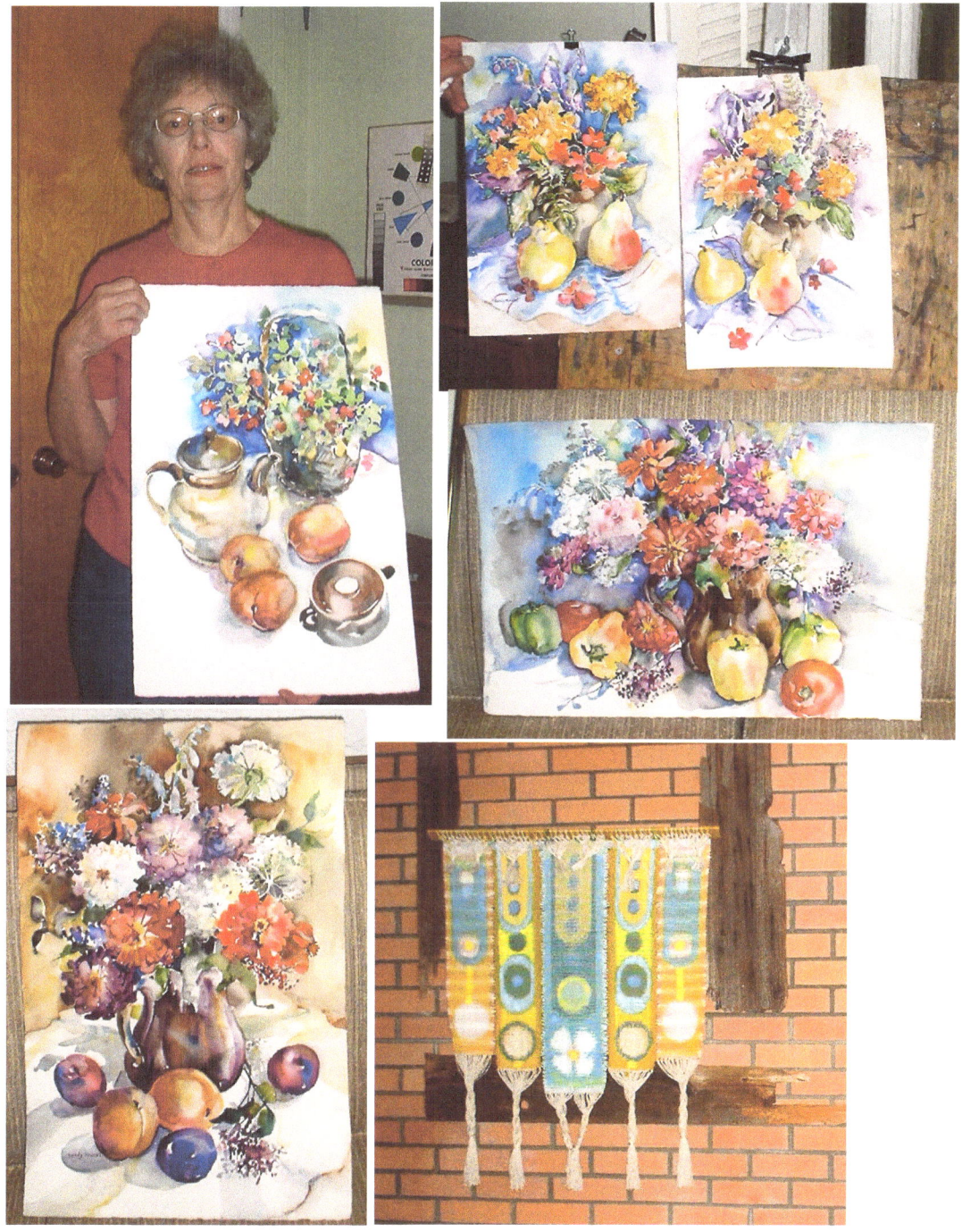

Sandy is now involved in setting up showings at the South Central Kentucky Cultural Center in Glasgow, KY and she has just arranged for a showing of the art of the Scottsville Art Society. You can also see Sandy's personal work at the Cultural Center in Glasgow or you can call her at 270 651 3610 to purchase any of her work.

Meet Kentucky artist Clarence Fredericks

Does anyone remember the Great Kentucky Watercolor Workshop Series? Well, the man who created, organized and presented them for 10 years was watercolorist Clarence Fredericks.

Clarence, a native of Ohio came to work at the now defunct Sorenson Corporation. He quietly lives in Glasgow KY.

His love of watercolors inspired him to create the workshops. His wife says

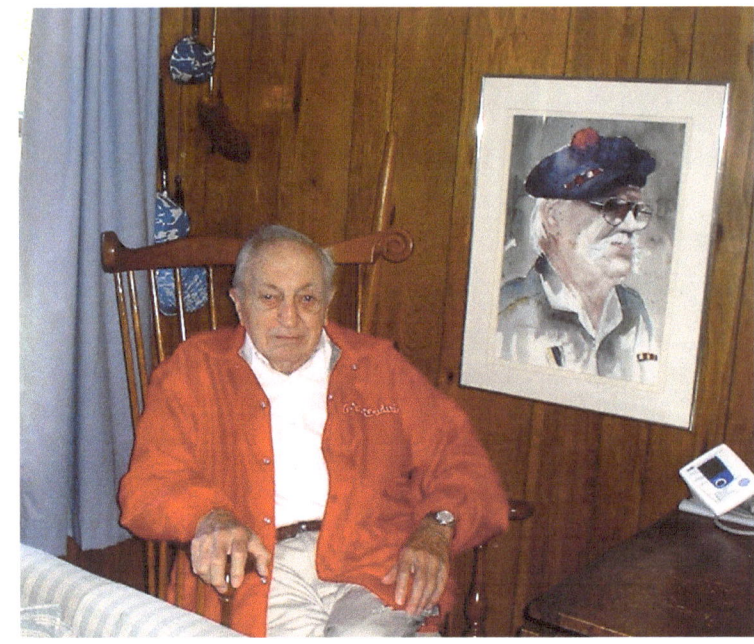

when they are at art shows or museums he will look at nothing but the watercolors! Their home is host to many brilliant water color paintings by many well known artists.

Clarence is no mean watercolorist himself. He says he never made on money on the workshop series and he was glad to break even. However, he got to attend each one and get to know all the famous watercolorists such as Tony Couch, Tom Lynch, Don Andrews, and Joe Fettings just to name a few of the 20 famous artists he was able to involve in this venture.

Clarence says he met Joe Fettings when he worked in Chicago and he encouraged Fettings to come to Kentucky to do a workshop, hence the start of the series which went on for 10 years. He did a spring, summer, and fall series.

Most of all his paintings are framed and covered in glass so it was just about impossible for me to get pictures of them. However, the picture of Clarence shows him seated next to one of his paintings. When I asked him how he started painting, he said that about 30 or 40 years ago he just started out on a Saturday afternoon painting in watercolors and has kept it up ever since. He used to paint mostly landscapes, farm scenes and barns, and then graduated into flowers and some portraits. His most famous painting is the Glasgow Court House. He has sold 20 of these paintings plus a series of landscapes.

Many people would see Clarence painting all over town as he really enjoyed painting Plein Air. He just loved the vibrancy of it and his work shows it. His advice to anyone who paints is just to keep at it, learn by doing and attend as many workshops as you can. It was indeed a privilege and a pleasure to meet this fine old gentleman and his lovely wife, Marge. Not only is his work brilliant, but his efforts to the art community over the years was indeed valuable.

Meet Kentucky artist Betty Brogan

I never realized there were so many amazing artists in our part of the world. Nor did I ever realize how popular water color painting has become again. To add to that, I never even thought that so many Kentucky artists would be so brilliantly talented.

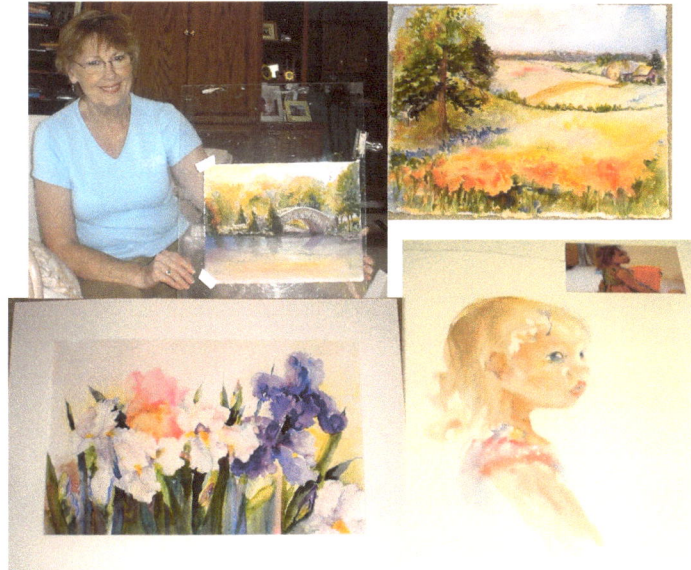
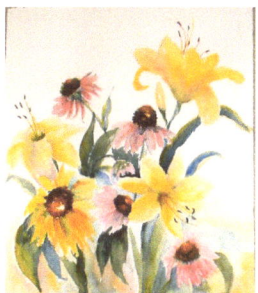

Betty Brogan with
Some of her work.

Well I have found another one and her name is Betty Brogan. Betty is a native of Kentucky, born in Harlan County, but raised in Hart County. She resides in Glasgow, KY with her retired husband.

A graduate of Union college and a retired executive assistant of the Chamber of Commerce, Betty is a self taught watercolorist who just "took to it" as she says. She also says her mentor and inspiration is artist Jane Kehrt. She loves attending Jane's watercolor classes.

Betty also goes to professional art workshops given by well known artists whenever she can. As an avid gardener, her work is inspired by the flowers and gardens she sees in the surrounding area. Though flowers are her favorite subjects, she is branching out into portraits and landscapes. Betty thoroughly enjoys Plein Air painting. She creates lovely post cards and note cards from her paintings which she sells. While interviewing her, one of her paintings sold at the Cultural Center in Glasgow proving she is a popular artist.

Her fondest wish would be to travel and to paint. Her advice to new painters "is to not be afraid to do it. It is 90% desire and 10% talent."

You can reach Betty Brogan at 270 678 5636 to purchase any of her artwork that is not on display at the Cultural Center or to buy any of her post cards or note cards.

Meet Kentucky artist Steve Clay

When does a drawing look almost like a photograph? When it is done by Summer Shade, KY artist Steve Clay!

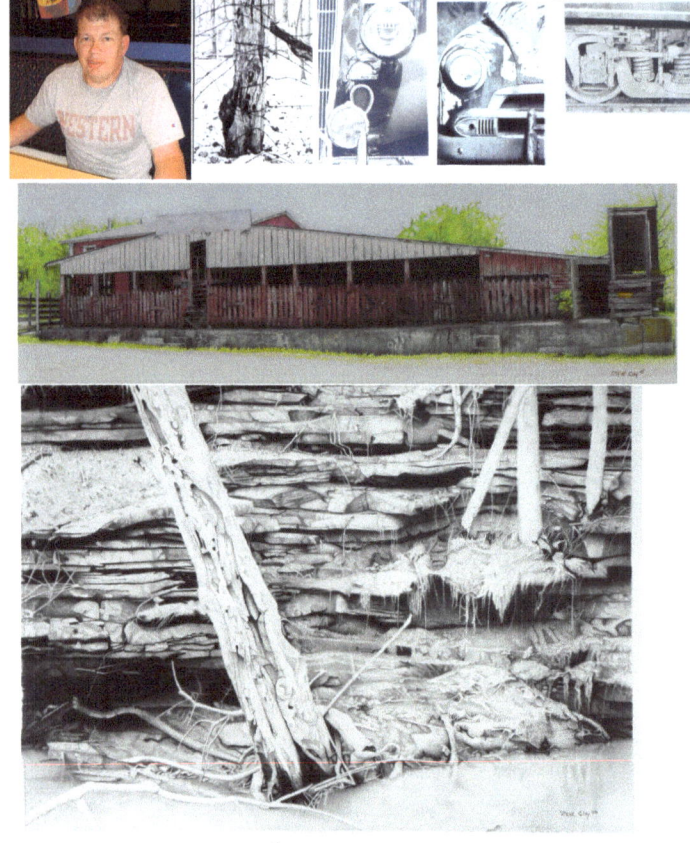

Shy and retiring, Steve Clay has been drawing since high school. He is so good at it that he won scholarships to several colleges and turned them down simply because he is shy. Steve started drawing fences, landscapes, posts, barns, cars, license plates; you name it when it dawned on him that instead of drawing the whole subject he might just zero in on a part of it that interested him. Thus he started to develop an incredible style that has brought him to the attention of many people. He won 1st place in the 2005 KY State Fair Purchase award with his tree stump and wire drawing. Another one of his drawings took 2nd place at the KY state fair. His drawing titled "51 on 31" will be high lighted in North Light's new drawing book titled "Stokes of Genius' Best Drawings"

There is a lot of interesting lines in a drawing that shows just the undercarriage of a train he saw at the L &M depot in Bowling Green, KY. Steve says most of his drawings have 100 to 150 hours of work in them and that he uses the finest graphic and colored pencils he can buy. He says he gets lost in his drawings and sketches and when he looks up thinking he has worked about 15 minutes he will discover he has been at it for 2 or 3 hours.

This writer believes that Steve Clay is just starting to come into his own as an artist and predicts his work will soon become really best sellers in the art world. His work starts at $500.00 and I personally feel that is dirt cheap! He can be reached at 670 6169 when he is not working as a machine operator at Dana Corporation. His dream is to be able to work at just drawing some day and be able to live on the signed limited edition prints from 4 or 5 works a year. This writer believes that with the right moves and help that could soon become a reality for Steve Clay. You can see some of his work at the Cultural Center in Glasgow, KY.

Meet Kentucky artist Jewelry creator Jill Gentry

Jill Gentry lives in Glasgow, KY and is a wire jewelry designer and creator. Though she has been doing it for only a little over a year her work is brilliantly professional and eye catching.

Jill says she decided this was something she wanted to do so she went to study with one of the best wire jewelry designer and creator in the country and that is Dale Armstrong over in Calhoun, TN. She says it was an expensive investment not only in time, but in money.

She learned to craft and repair bracelets, earrings, pins, chains, rings, and watches. One needs to also develop skills in sawing, filing, soldering,

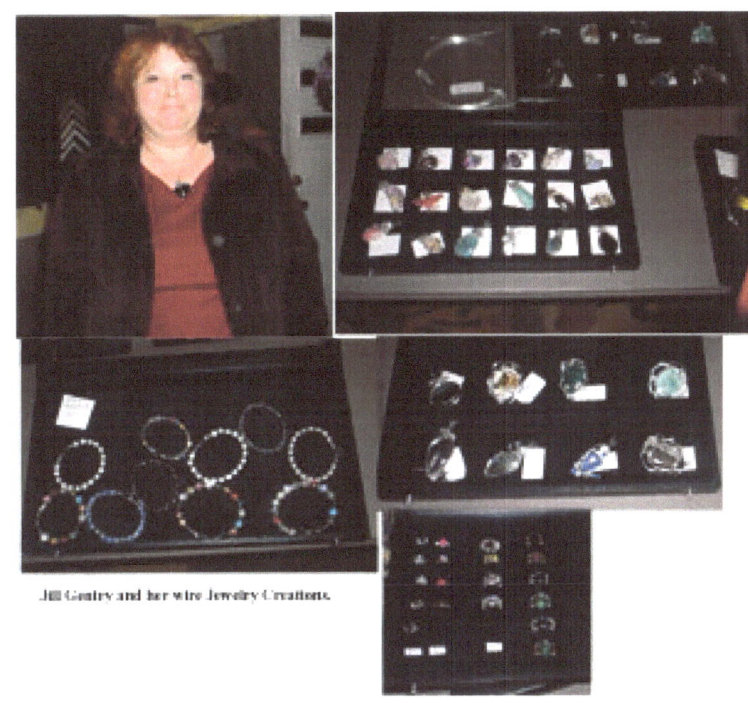

Jill Gentry and her wire Jewelry Creations.

pickling, cleaning, piercing, polishing, forging, embossing, engraving, casting, enameling, laminating, and working with gemstones and metals.

Wire jewelry crafting in complicated and takes skill, patience and a good eye for design. It is time consuming though the finished piece looks amazingly simple. However, one needs to know what kind of wire to use. Gold, silver or copper, should it be hard or soft wire since wire comes in three different forms of hardness: dead soft, half-hard, and full-hard.

Dead Soft is very soft and can be bent with your hands. It is often used for wire-sculpted jewelry. Half-Hard wire is harder than dead soft wire because it has been pulled through a draw plate (a tool with holes in it the same size and shape of the wire). Full-Hard wire is harder than half-hard wire because it has been pulled through a draw plate more times than half-hard wire.

Wire comes in a variety of shapes such as round, square, and half-round. In the US, the size or thickness of wire is measured in gauge (also spelt gage) while in most European countries they measure it in millimeters. For instance 26 – 24 gauge (.40mm - .50mm) – This size is good for beads that have small holes in them such as pearls. In an ounce of 26 gauge wire there is about 76 feet and in 24 gauge there is about 48 feet of wire and in 22 – 21 gauge (.65mm - .71mm) are both very versatile sizes because they are pretty thick but most beads (like crystals and stone beads) can fit on them. One ounce of 22 gauge has about 31 feet and 21 gauges has about 24 feet of wire. Then there is 20 gauges (.80mm) – This is about the thickest wire and it's good for making clasps because it's still pretty easy to work with but is strong as well. Most crafters usually buy this in dead soft. You can get about 19 feet of 20 gauge wire when you buy it by the ounce.

One can use copper wire in projects because it looks nice with some designs that use earth tone colors. Copper will darken and discolor with age, which is called a patina affect. If you prefer to keep your copper wire bright, you can simply polish it.

You can use and find galvanized wire (along with copper wire) in most hardware stores. It is a dull silver color and is also good practice wire. This wire is harder than the silver wire you may be used to, so get a small gauge if you plan to get some. Sterling silver wire sterling wire works the best for many of my finished jewelry pieces. Sterling indicates that the wire is 92.5% pure silver. The rest is made up of alloys (such as copper or zinc) to provide strength. Sterling will tarnish, called oxidation, so it's best to keep in zip lock bags or sealed containers of some kind when not using it for jewelry or wearing the jewelry itself. When it does tarnish (and it eventually will), you can polish by using a polishing kit, using a magnetic polisher or tumbler, or you can clean it with an ionic cleaner.

Fine silver wire is made of 99.9% pure silver, many wire workers enjoy working with fine silver. Fine silver is softer than sterling. Since it has fewer alloys, it also does not tarnish as quickly as sterling silver does. Gold filled wire is never called "gold wire." since gold-filed metal has many layers of gold, it is not pure gold. On the upside, gold-filled is of much better quality than plated gold (only one layer) so gold-filled lasts for a very long time if cared for properly. It is a wonderful alternative to gold, which is pretty expensive! However, a wire jewelry creator can offer real gold wire in various karats (10-24 for example) and even different colors. Last, but not least, you have coated color wires which is coated with an enamel to create the color of the wire. This wire has become very popular and is even available in many large craft stores.

People like Jill Gentry then use stones, semi-precious gems, and precious gems to wrap their chosen wire around thus creating a beautiful pendant, earring set, rings, pins or bracelets.

Her prices start at $35.00 and go up to $120.00 for something like a beautiful white spinal pendant with a ruby insert she just created. Jill is getting ready for a one time pre-Christmas show at her home studio and you can find out more about it by calling her at 270 678 7192

Meet Kentucky artist Connie Irene Demunbrun

Connie Irene Demunbrun, a native of Warren County now lives in Franklin, KY. The first part of her family came over from France and settled in Nashville TN where there is a street named after them. Now add the fact that Connie is a kin of Daniel Boone and you get a pretty interesting person who just happens to be a full time artist.

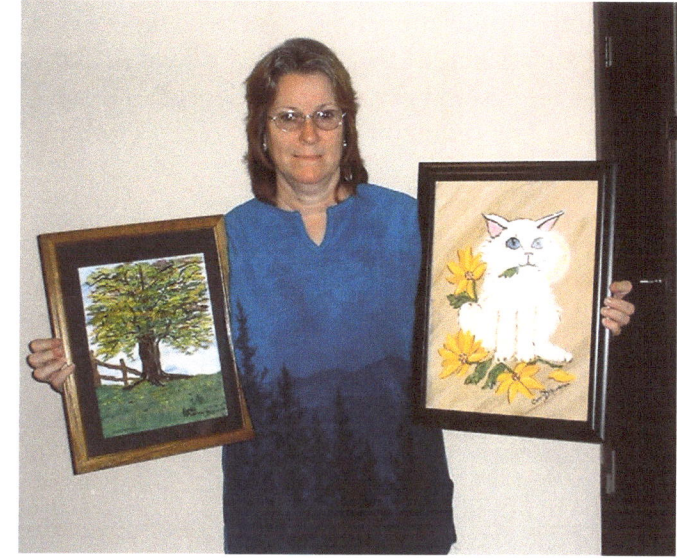

Connie works out of her home studio and is an artist in watercolors and pencils as she is allergic to some of the properties in oil paints. She has been working in art since she was about 10 years old.

Connie says both her daughters, ages 23 and 29, are artistically inclined but do not apply themselves to that field.

When I asked Connie what her one wish in the art field would be she did not hesitate with her answer. "I would like to meet some like-minded artists who would want to share the rent in a downtown Bowling Green, KY art Gallery/studio."

Well, here is an opportunity for some artists with the same idea. Just call Connie at 270 598 4995 or email her at demunbrunc@bellsouth.net. For those of you interested in viewing Connie's art give her a call also.

Meet Kentucky artist C. David Jones

C. David Jones decided he wanted to paint 100 of the same subject. He did not know what the subject would be, he just knew he wanted to be 100 paintings of the same subject and that subject turned out to be avocados! You can go to the Capital Arts Alliance Inc. at 416 East Main St. in Bowling Green KY and be awed, amazed and dumbfounded at the sight of 100 paintings of a half of an avocado.

David is a native of Glasgow, KY and is a partner in LOT 916 Gallery. His murals have been commissioned in Chicago and across western Kentucky in private homes and public spaces.

Most recently, he completed a large mural for Western Kentucky University and will be working on a second there soon. Mariah's Restaurant, a historic location in downtown Bowling Green has several of David's murals. His work has been purchased by Mammoth Cave National Park's permanent collection. This artist earned his undergraduate degree from Centre College in Danville, KY., and Masters of Fine Arts degree from Savannah College in Georgia. He was awarded one of the prestigious Kentucky Arts Council's Individual Artist's Fellowships.

David is an adjunct professor at Western, teaching drawing and art education. His paintings include work derived from the typical family album with a regional flare. David will gladly discuss doing a special commission for you!

C. David Jones with some of his
100 Avocado paintings & other art.

When I asked him at what point did he get tired of painting 100 avocados he said never. He looked forward to going into his studio every day and working and he says he felt quite sad when he finished the last painting. When I asked him if he had carte blanch to do anything in the whole world he quickly said, "To work in my studio daily". As a prolific artist, David creates a lot of art besides the 100 avocados and he says his favorite piece was done about 5 years ago and was a painting of a woman with a suitcase standing in front of a Waffle House. He works in all mediums and his favorite type of art is doing public murals.

Their first studio, Lot 916, originated in downtown Bowling Green Kentucky's Fountain Square and was owned and operated by Kim and David Jones along with jewelry designer Mitsy Clendenin from 1998 to 2006. In April of 2006, the couple moved the location to their renovated Italianate on State Street which they call Jones' for Art. Kim and David continue to show the best in regional, original artists through special event openings. Mitsy's jewelry design, aka MC Design Group, can be found at better shops throughout the mid-South and by special order. Both Kim and David, along with daughter Marlee, make their works available on a regular basis through LOT 916 Home Studio. David's words of wisdom to all artists are simply this. "Be prolific." You can view his work, along with his wife Kim and their 12 year old daughter Marlee at the both galleries. His phone number is 270 783 9080 and their website is www.lot916.com .

Meet Kentucky artist Margaret Bevarly

Margaret Bevarly of Smiths Grove, KY says being 77 years old has not slowed her down in the least when it comes to being a transparent watercolorist.

Like many artists, Margaret says she has been dabbling all her life. However, it wasn't until the early 70's that she entered into her first art show. "Prior to that most of my paintings went under the bed", she says.

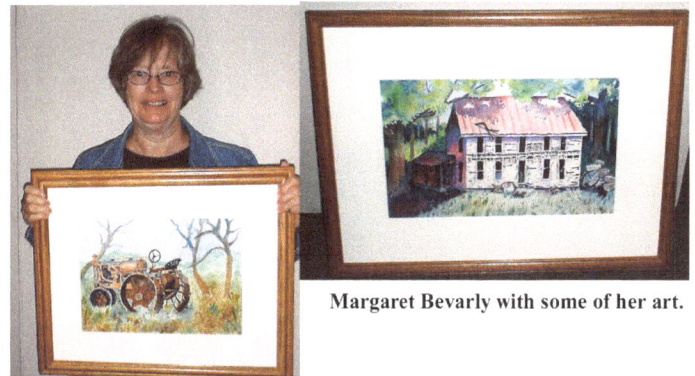

Margaret Bevarly with some of her art.

Transparent watercolors have no black or white and are quite difficult to make successfully. The specific term watercolor refers to paintings done on a special rag paper with pigments very finely ground in a binding medium composed of a solution of gum Arabic. Watercolor paintings are done in a thin, transparent manner; pale tones are obtained by dilution of the paint with water thus producing such a thin layer of pigment that the brilliant white effect of the paper is mingled with the color. This method of coloring generally is called the transparent or glaze system, and it is entirely different from the other coloring method called the opaque or body-color system

Margaret has mastered this technique well and from time to time has won many art awards. She started out in oils, but she was introduced to watercolors she says through a romance when an 80 year old man married a 70 year old gal and decided to give a class in watercolors.

Margaret has a home studio that has progressed over the years from a kitchen table to a sewing room to finally one of her children's bedroom after they moved from home. She sells her paintings mostly in a ¼ sheet and the prices range from $250.00 to $300.00. One can make an appointment by calling Margaret at 270 563 3291 to view her work.

Margaret says she cannot improve upon working at her simple drafting table and her brush in hand is total contentment. Her advice to other artists just beginning is to just do it and don't get discouraged!

Meet Kentucky artist Kim Jones

Kim Jones, a Bowling Green, KY artist is also a native of Springfield TN. Besides being a full time artist is also a free lance commercial and set designer, full time mother of 12 year old Marlee Jones (a successful young artist in her own right), wife of artist C. David Jones and business partner of both Lot 916 and Jones'n for Art Galleries in Bowling

Green, KY seemed quite unflustered as streams of people came in and out of their State St. Gallery this past Saturday morning.

Kim has a Fine Arts Degree, a BFA in Graphic Design and a 2 year degree in business which helps out a lot because she handles a lot of business for the family.

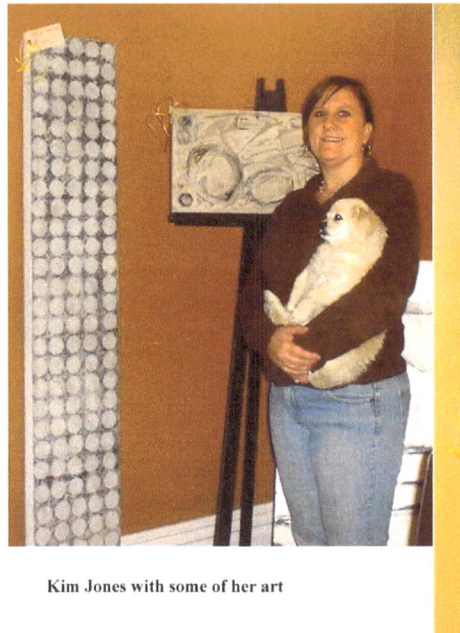

Kim Jones with some of her art

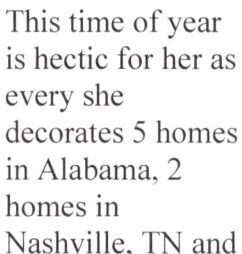

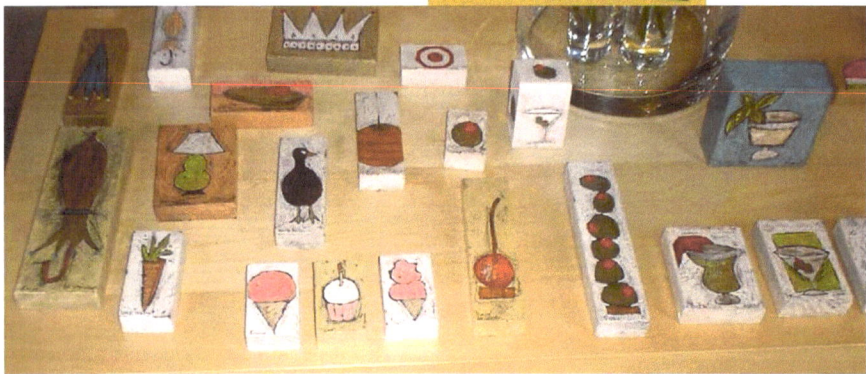

Currently she and her family are rehabbing the State St. Gallery and bringing a condemned building back to life as not only their family business, but their family home. She says she has always had a home studio and she likes that just fine.

This time of year is hectic for her as every she decorates 5 homes in Alabama, 2 homes in Nashville, TN and other clients homes here for their Christmas decorations.

Kim likes working in acrylics and mixed media stuff she says and she feels she has the best of all worlds by having a job that is fun.

Her work is whimsical in her small wood pieces and profound in her larger pieces. Kim advises other artists to think about what you love and do it with a passion.

You can view her work on line at www.Lot916.com or visit either studio in Bowling Green, KY. Their phone number is 270 783 9080.

Meet Kentucky artist Marlee Jones

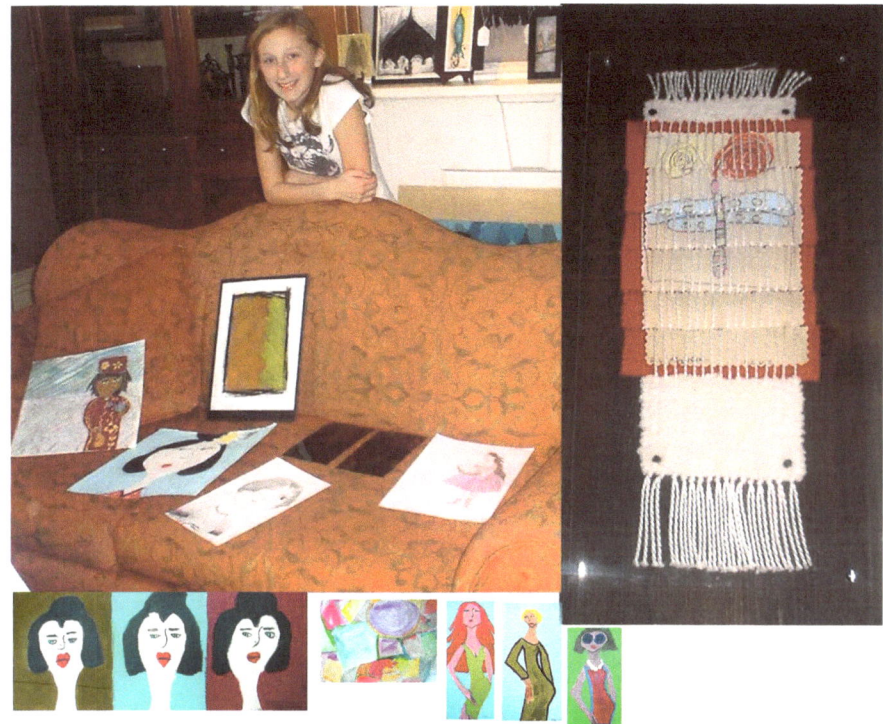

Marlee Jones, at the time of this writing, is a 12 year old artist and a native of Bowling Green, KY. She says she loves being the daughter of two artists because they have a good eye and they are fun people. She is not hampered by having both parents as artists because they have encouraged her to find her own style. Marlee has taken the tools of her parents and fashioned things her way. You can find her most days side by side with her father C. David Jones in his studio.

Marlee says she has always loved to draw and painted her first big piece when she was about 5 years old.

It was a pleasure doing this interview with this bright 12 year old. She has a clear mind and clear responses to my questions. Her analytical outlook to art seemed to be that of someone older. Marlee is more fortunate than most school children today who are students in programs that are dedicated to "leaving no child behind". With most schools focusing on math and reading, creative and imaginative youngsters are the ones who are being left behind because today's school budgets do not allow much for the arts of any kinds. It is a shame that the narrowing of curriculum is at the expense of other kinds of learning like the arts, science, history and foreign language seems to be shortchanging our children's future.

It does not seem to be a problem for this little 7th grader as Marlee's world is full of the things that other children may not be exposed to. Besides the art, she likes to collect Troll dolls and skate board. She says she loves the feel of the wind on her face and in her hair. She enjoys her pets Chase and Max, 2 well mannered little dogs.

Marlee focuses on the abstract art and many of her pieces have sold and she feels good about that by stating, "I think people see what I see in my art when it is completed."

Abstract art is now generally understood to mean art that does not depict objects in the natural world, but instead uses color and form in a non-representational or subjective way. In the very early 20th century, the term was more often used to describe art, such as Cubist and Futurist art, that depicts real forms in a simplified or rather reduced way, keeping only an allusion of the original natural subject. Such paintings were often claimed to capture something of the depicted objects' immutable intrinsic qualities rather than its external appearance. The term "non-figurative art" is sometimes used synonymously with abstraction.

Her goal is to major in art and to have fun doing it. Her words of wisdom to other kids are, "Don't say you can't paint or draw. No one is good or bad at it. It simply looks different." She says she urges all kids to just do it.

Marlee doesn't like it when people judge the artist by what the artist paints. She likes that art is "hands on". She says people should study art history, such as Van Gogh, but then tries to paint in his style for awhile as that will help them develop their own style.

You can see more of Marlee's work at her website www.Lot916.com or at her parent's two galleries in Bowling Green, KY. Lot916 on the Square or at Jones's for Art at 1252 State St.
Marlee's past Shows:
Chamber Of Commerce, Bowling Green KY; August 1 -31, 2005
Capitol Arts Alliance Mezzanine Gallery, Bowling Green, Kentucky as part of "The Family Business" May 2005 show.
International Festival Gallery Walk; Participant Sept. 16, 2005
World's Greatest Studio Tour and Art Sale Nov. 4 & 5, 2006, Bowling Green and Alvaton, KY

Should you wish to be in the 2007 or any future upcoming editions of Who's Who in KY Arts and Crafts©, just email the author at askarlene@scrtc.com and put Who's Who in KY Arts and Crafts in the subject line or call me at 270 524 9567 It's Free!